The Role of Incentives in Investment Promotion

TRENDS AND PRACTICES IN OECD MEMBER COUNTRIES

OECD
BETTER POLICIES FOR BETTER LIVES

Please cite this publication as:
OECD (2024), *The Role of Incentives in Investment Promotion: Trends and Practices in OECD Member Countries*, OECD Publishing, Paris, https://doi.org/10.1787/e3338264-en.

ISBN 978-92-64-38859-8 (print)
ISBN 978-92-64-74747-0 (PDF)
ISBN 978-92-64-34577-5 (HTML)

Photo credits: Cover © Nutthaseth Vanchaichana/Getty Images.

Corrigenda to OECD publications may be found at: https://www.oecd.org/en/publications/support/corrigenda.html.

Foreword

This report presents a comparative analysis of trends and practices of investment incentives across OECD member countries, focusing on their role within broader investment promotion strategies. Governments use tax and non-tax incentives to attract investment, particularly foreign direct investment (FDI), targeting specific sectors and locations to support national development goals. While investment incentives are often a key component of countries' investment promotion strategies, the role and responsibilities of investment promotion agencies (IPAs) varies significantly across jurisdictions.

The report aims to explore how different incentives function within the wider context of investment promotion and facilitation. The first part examines the policy objectives behind investment incentives in OECD countries, the types of incentives offered, their design processes and key features. The second part discusses the importance of incentives within investment promotion strategies, and the involvement of IPAs in their design, governance and management.

The report draws extensively on data collected from the 2024 *OECD Survey on Investment Promotion and Investment Incentives*, conducted with all 35 national IPAs in the OECD. It also draws on existing literature and reflects the classifications and priorities elaborated through the joint work of the OECD Investment Division and the OECD Centre for Tax Policy and Administration on investment incentives. While OECD IPAs may not be directly responsible for designing or granting incentives, they often have detailed knowledge of available incentives as part of their investment promotion strategies. Some are also involved in shaping incentive policies through advocacy efforts. However, this does not necessarily mean they have a comprehensive understanding of all incentives offered nationwide. Responses from OECD IPAs provide insights on trends and practices regarding investment incentives in investment promotion, but not necessarily a comprehensive inventory of all incentives in each jurisdiction.

The report was prepared by Alexandre de Crombrugghe and Juan Felipe Rodrigo from the Investment Division in the OECD Directorate for Financial and Enterprise Affairs, under the overall guidance of Ana Novik, Head of the Investment Division. It benefitted from inputs and comments from Katharina Böhm, Taufeeq Nihal Khan, Fernando Mistura and Martin Wermelinger from the Investment Division as well as Sarah Dayan, Luisa Dressler and Clara Gascon from the Tax Policy and Statistics Division in the OECD Centre for Tax Policy and Administration. Meral Gedik and Lucinda Pearson prepared it for publication and Angèle N'zinga provided administrative assistance. The report has been conducted under the Work Programme of the OECD IPA Network and was used as background paper for the ninth OECD IPA Network Meeting on 5 November 2024. The report also aims to bring the investment promotion perspective to broader horizontal OECD work exploring how to improve the design, governance, evaluation and monitoring of investment incentives for advancing sustainable objectives and maximising net benefits.

The report was submitted to the OECD Investment Committee for comments on 22 October 2024 and then declassified by the Investment Committee on 6 December 2024.

The report has been financially supported by the full members of the OECD IPA Network.

Table of contents

Foreword 3

Abbreviations and acronyms 6

Executive summary 7

1 Investment incentives in the OECD: Key features and objectives 9
- 1.1. Definition and rationale for investment incentives 10
- 1.2. Objectives, types and legal framework of investment incentives 13
- 1.3. Design and scope of investment incentives 20
- 1.4. Sector and location-based targeting of investment incentives 26
- Note 29

2 The role of incentives in promoting investment: Strategic importance for IPAs and institutional implications 30
- 2.1. Investment incentives within IPAs' investment promotion strategies 31
- 2.2. The role of IPAs in the governance of investment incentives 39
- Note 49

References 50

FIGURES

Figure 1.1. Investment incentives in OECD countries typically aim to enhance productivity and innovation, but also target specific goals such as regional development and job creation 14
Figure 1.2. Within tax incentives, OECD countries predominantly grant CIT incentives, particularly expenditure-based incentives credits and allowances 16
Figure 1.3. Financial incentives dominate the non-tax investment incentive spectrum 17
Figure 1.4. Legal frameworks and information accessibility for investment incentives tend to be scattered 19
Figure 1.5. Business actors are highly consulted in the design of incentives 21
Figure 1.6. Benchmarking other countries' incentive schemes is a common practice in the OECD 22
Figure 1.7. OECD countries often determine financial benefits using quantitative parameters and expert assessment 23
Figure 1.8. In most jurisdictions, investment incentives are contingent upon the size of the investment 24
Figure 1.9. Investment incentives are generally unrestricted in terms of firm size, ownership or origin 25
Figure 1.10. Location-based conditions are frequently used in OECD incentives, often targeting remote or underdeveloped areas 26
Figure 1.11. Sector-based incentives target the green and digital transitions, aligning with OECD IPA priorities 27
Figure 1.12. OECD IPAs typically focus on multiple sectors for investment promotion 29
Figure 2.1. OECD incentive schemes often align with the strategic objectives and priority sectors of IPAs 31

Figure 2.2. Limited overlap between sector-specific incentives and IPA prioritised sectors highlights need for better co-ordination 32
Figure 2.3. IPAs from smaller economies tend to place greater importance on incentives in investment location decisions 34
Figure 2.4. The GMT is not expected to prompt major changes in IPA promotion strategies 38
Figure 2.5. OECD IPAs focus more on providing information, advocacy and advice than on designing and granting incentives 40
Figure 2.6. A higher number of incentives-related functions performed by IPAs is associated with a greater importance placed on incentives 41
Figure 2.7. Investors typically need to engage with multiple actors to apply for investment incentives, while IPA roles differ across jurisdictions 42
Figure 2.8. In decentralised countries, subnational authorities tend to have a greater degree of involvement in the governance of incentives 43
Figure 2.9. While subnational incentives are rarely offered in co-ordination with national incentives, subnational authorities are often involved in the granting of incentives 44
Figure 2.10. The co-ordination of IPAs with government entities is mostly informal, both at national and subnational levels 45
Figure 2.11. IPAs tend to participate less in M&E activities compared to other government agencies and ministries 48

TABLES

Table 1.1. Tax incentives typology 10
Table 1.2. Investment incentives offered across OECD countries 15
Table 1.3. Sector-specific conditions in incentives and the prioritisation of sectors by IPAs are common practices among OECD countries. 28
Table 2.1. IPAs tend to consider that incentives are not a deciding factor for investment location 33
Table 2.2. IPAs tend to rank the provision of incentives lower than other factors in attracting firms across different types of investments 35
Table 2.3. Incentives are relatively less important compared to other measures undertaken by OECD IPAs in their promotion strategies 36
Table 2.4. Participation of IPAs in incentive co-ordination mechanisms with government entities 46

BOXES

Box 1.1. The OECD Survey on Investment Promotion and Investment Incentives 10
Box 1.2. OECD ongoing work on investment incentives 12
Box 1.3. Improving transparency of incentives for investment facilitation 20
Box 1.4. Green Corridor for Large-Scale Investment Projects Multiple target 24
Box 2.1. Beyond incentives: Innovative measures for to promote investment in selected OECD countries 36
Box 2.2. IPA centralised process for the granting of investment incentives: the example of Poland 42
Box 2.3. US states business incentives database and target industries dashboard 44
Box 2.4. CzechInvest Dashboard on Investment incentives Statistics 47

Abbreviations and acronyms

BEPS	Base Erosion and Profit Shifting
CAPEX	Capital expenditures
CIT	Corporate income tax
EU	European Union
ETR	Effective tax rate
FDI	Foreign direct investment
GloBE	Global Anti-Base Erosion Model Rules
GMT	Global Minimum Tax
ICT	Information & communication technology
IPA	Investment promotion agency
KPI	Key performance indicators
M&E	Monitoring and evaluation
MNE	Multinational enterprise
OECD	Organisation for Economic Co-operation and Development
R&D	Research and development
SDGs	Sustainable Development Goals
SEZs	Special economic zones
SMEs	Small and medium sized enterprises
SOEs	State-owned enterprises

Executive summary

Governments around the world have widely deployed tax and non-tax incentives to attract investors in specific sectors and locations and support national development objectives (OECD, 2022[1]). OECD countries are no exception: according to the survey results, all 35 national OECD IPAs report that their governments employ at least one investment incentive to attract or retain foreign investment, with tax incentives being used by 97% of countries. OECD countries use a combination of tax and non-tax incentives. Corporate income tax (CIT) incentives are reported to be significantly more prevalent than other tax incentives, with 86% of OECD countries offering them. Non-tax incentives are dominated by financial incentives, such as grant, subsidies and loans, which are also offered in 86% of OECD jurisdictions. Regulatory incentives are less common, available about half of jurisdictions, while in-kind benefits are provided in just below a third of countries.

The rationale for offering incentives is to attract investments that might not otherwise occur as well as aligning these efforts with governments' objectives like capital attraction, job creation, productivity enhancement, and sustainable development. By bridging the gap between private profitability and public interest, incentives serve targeted policy goals beyond merely promoting and facilitating investment. For instance, three-quarters of OECD countries consider that enhancing productivity and innovation is a top objective of their incentive regime, while promoting regional development and job creation are top objectives behind incentives in approximately half of OECD countries and addressing climate change in just below a third. Other sustainable development goals, such as gender equality, social inclusion, and export promotion, are less important objectives behind investment incentives, according to respondents.

The regulatory frameworks governing these incentives are complex and fragmented, often involving multiple overlapping legal structures. Most countries (86%) primarily rely on tax laws to govern tax incentives, which are nonetheless frequently also governed by other legal instruments. Non-tax incentives are often regulated by multiple competing frameworks, with 54% of OECD countries using supranational legislation, just below half relying on investment laws, and about a third on subnational or sector-specific laws. This lack of consolidation can create challenges for public governance, scrutiny, and transparency regarding the costs and benefits of incentives. For investors, navigating these scattered and intricate frameworks can be time-consuming and may limit access to the full range of incentive schemes.

The design of incentives is often shaped by external factors, creating pressure to sustain their use. For example, 80% of IPAs report that international competition influences incentive design, suggesting that the eligibility criteria of incentives and their benefits may be offered to match those of other countries. Additionally, public consultations are integral to incentive design, with 91% of OECD countries incorporating insights primarily from private sector actors, while engagement with academia and civil society is less common.

When it comes to eligibility for incentives, investment size conditions – such as minimum amounts invested or jobs created – are used by 83% of countries. However, three-quarters of OECD jurisdictions do not differentiate between foreign and domestic investors, or between large and small firms, in their incentive policies. Most OECD countries also allow state-owned enterprises to apply for investment incentives, ensuring broad access across various types of firms.

Similarly, sectoral and regional targeting are central strategies in OECD incentive design, with 77% of countries focusing on specific industries and 91% on particular locations. While climate change and the digital transition are not reported as the most pressing policy objectives behind incentives, the sectors targeted by incentives still focus highly on these areas. Priority sectors include those aligned with the climate and digital transitions, such as renewable energy (66%), battery production (57%), and semiconductors (51%). Location-based incentives are also widespread, with two-thirds of OECD countries specifically targeting remote or less developed regions to bolster regional development objectives.

Despite their wide use across OECD member countries, IPAs generally do not consider incentives, especially tax incentives, as critical factors in influencing investor location decisions. CIT incentives score a relevance rating of 5.3/10, and other tax incentives 4.7/10, while non-tax incentives are seen as somewhat more important (6.5/10). This is not uniformly the case across OECD countries, however, as IPAs in smaller economies consider incentives more influential. Broadly, OECD IPAs see incentives as just one of many factors in attracting investment. Infrastructure quality, workforce skills, and a supportive legal environment are considered more crucial, regardless of the type of incentives – tax or non-tax – or the type of investment – natural resource-seeking, export-oriented, or market-seeking. IPAs thus take a multifaceted approach to attract FDI, with incentives being just one component of their broader offering to investors. In contrast, activities related to image-building, investment facilitation, and investment generation are regarded as more important than promoting and offering investment incentives.

OECD IPAs report incentives to be aligned with their strategic objectives in 83% of cases and with their priority sectors in 71% of them. Nonetheless, IPAs typically do not participate in incentive design, which is handled by ministries or other agencies. Tax incentives fall under the jurisdiction of tax authorities and finance ministries, while non-tax incentives often have multiple governing authorities. While IPAs can play various roles in managing both tax and non-tax incentives, they are active in overseeing non-tax incentives in 38% of cases compared to just 23% for tax incentives.

OECD countries use various institutional arrangements to manage investment incentive applications, affecting the number of entities investors must interact with. While IPAs play a leading or secondary role in the governance of incentives in 70% of cases, other institutions are often involved as well. Two-thirds of IPAs report that ministries, such as those for economic affairs, industry, trade, or specific sectors, are the main counterparts for investors, while finance ministries lead in fewer than 10% of cases. Investors must interact with multiple entities at national and subnational levels, risking adding complexity and time to the process. A centralised system, with a single point of contact, could simplify the application process for investors.

In decentralised countries, subnational authorities typically have a greater role in the governance of investment incentives. Subnational incentives are available in 83% of OECD jurisdictions and can be offered either in co-ordination with, or independently of, national incentives. In federal or more decentralised countries, subnational authorities typically assume more roles, such as evaluating applications, awarding incentives, overseeing compliance, and developing policies. Whereas in unitary or more centralised countries, subnational authorities have a more limited involvement in these activities.

Although IPAs work with both national and subnational bodies, much of this collaboration is informal, which can limit the effectiveness of incentive implementation. Since investment is a horizontal policy affecting multiple institutions, effective co-ordination mechanisms are needed to align policy goals and ensure that investment incentives are implemented effectively. Formalising these co-ordination efforts could enhance the efficiency of incentives and improve alignment across different levels of government.

Monitoring and evaluation (M&E) of investment incentives are also areas where IPAs have a limited role. While other government agencies participate in nearly 90% of M&E activities, IPAs engage in these processes only about half the time. Their main role often involves collecting investor feedback (57%), which complements the broader government assessment on the use and effectiveness of incentives.

1 Investment incentives in the OECD: Key features and objectives

Investment incentives in OECD member countries vary in terms of their scope, targets, conditions, and policy objectives. To explore these issues, this chapter first defines the concept of investment incentives, introduces the OECD typology of incentives and discusses the rationale behind investment incentives through a brief literature review. It then examines the objectives and use of investment incentives across OECD IPAs drawing on data from the 2024 *OECD Survey on Investment Promotion and Investment Incentives*. The chapter further analyses the design of investment incentives, including stakeholder consultations, the role of international benchmarking, and approaches for determining financial benefits and their scope. Finally, it concludes with an overview of sectoral targeting in investment incentives.

1.1. Definition and rationale for investment incentives

Governments in OECD member countries use a range of tax and non-tax incentives as part of their investment attraction strategies. These incentives are tailored to specific industries, regions, and investment types, to attract FDI and achieve various policy objectives.

While there is no universally agreed definition of investment incentives, they are commonly understood as any form of specific advantage provided to certain investors or investment projects beyond what is available to all firms or projects in a jurisdiction (Celani, Dressler and Wermelinger, 2022[2]). Investment incentives are a key component of OECD governments' strategies for attracting investment. According to the OECD Survey on Investment Promotion and Investment Incentives (Box 1.1), all 35 participating IPAs highlight that their jurisdictions provide at least one investment incentive to promote or retain investment, reflecting that offering investment incentives is a widespread practice across OECD countries. Governments promote investment through a variety of policy instruments that they have at their disposal. However, investment incentives are not homogeneous in their policy objectives, in their scope or in the instruments used and include a broad variety of incentive instruments and design provisions (Celani, Dressler and Wermelinger, 2022[2]). They can take many forms, including tax, financial, regulatory, and in-kind incentives (Table 1.1).

Table 1.1. Tax incentives typology

Type	Description	Examples
Tax incentives	Investment incentives that affect government revenue collection, such as preferential treatment under tax and customs duties and other benefits	Corporate income tax, value added tax, customs and import duties
Financial incentives	Direct transfer of government funds, other government financing mechanisms or support.	Direct grants, subsidised loans, loan guarantees.
In-kind incentives	State provision of goods and services at below market value or for free, with an identifiable monetary value	Provision of land or infrastructure for specific projects or areas at below market value, such as in economic zones
Regulatory & non-financial incentives	Derogations from standard rules and regulations, some specialised regulations, specialised assistance and services, and other non-financial government support	Preferential standards and regulations, such as eased administrative requirements and procedures, administrative and regulatory exemptions

Source: Based on OECD (2023[3]), "Improving transparency of incentives for investment facilitation", *OECD Business and Finance Policy Papers*, No. 35, OECD Publishing, Paris, https://doi.org/10.1787/bf84ff64-en.

Box 1.1. The OECD Survey on Investment Promotion and Investment Incentives

In 2024, the OECD IPA Network is exploring various facets of investment incentives. It aims to offer a comparative overview of trends and practices across OECD member countries. For this purpose, a questionnaire was developed to collect data on the types, scopes and targets of incentives offered, their alignment with broader investment promotion and development objectives, and the governance and monitoring mechanisms used. The database does not capture an exhaustive list of existing incentives deployed by each jurisdiction, but rather provides an overview of trends and practices. It aims to provide a clearer understanding of how different incentives function within the broader context of investment promotion and facilitation.

The survey was shared with IPA representatives from OECD countries in the form of an online questionnaire, which was completed between June and July 2024 with a participation of all OECD countries that have a national IPA. The dataset includes national IPAs from the following 35 countries:

Australia, Austria, Canada, Chile, Colombia, Costa Rica, Czechia, Denmark, Estonia, Finland, France, Germany, Greece, Hungary, Iceland, Ireland, Italy, Japan, Korea, Latvia, Lithuania, Luxembourg, the Netherlands, New Zealand, Poland, Portugal, the Slovak Republic, Slovenia, Spain, Sweden, Switzerland, Türkiye, the United Kingdom, and the United States.

Note: Belgium, Israel, and Mexico are not represented in this analysis because they do not have a national IPA. For Italy, the responding institution was InvItalia, which is the national agency for inward investment and economic development, rather than ITA - Invest in Italy, a department of the Italian Trade Agency, which is more commonly known as the IPA.

Although prevalent among OECD countries, investment incentives represent only one element of a broader set of factors influencing investor decisions. Multinational enterprises (MNEs) often prioritise factors such as governance reforms, development of local suppliers, and investments in domestic infrastructure and human capital (James, 2013[4]; Danzman and Slaski, 2021[5]). Surveys, like those conducted by the World Bank on investment climate, consistently show that investors do not view incentives as decisive factors in their investment decisions (Tuomi, 2012[6]; World Bank Group, 2018[7]). Still, incentives often serve as a tiebreaker in the final stages of negotiations between investors and governments of shortlisted investment locations (Andersen, Kett and von Uexkull, 2018[8]). Therefore, governments may view incentives as necessary to compete with other countries to remain attractive given the global mobility of FDI (Tuomi, 2012[6]; James, 2013[4]).

Governments generally justify the use of investment incentives due to information asymmetries between investors and host governments (Harding and Javorcik, 2012[9]), as well as to compensate deficiencies in the investment climate (James, 2013[4]; Havránek and Iršová, 2010[10]). However, the efficacy and efficiency of these incentives remain contested. Research suggests that a significant proportion of firms benefiting from these incentives would have invested even without them, indicating potential inefficiencies. Tax incentives can also lead to substantial revenue losses for governments (OECD, 2021[11]). James (2013[4]) provides evidence that, in developing countries, 58–98% of firms that received incentives across different jurisdictions would have invested without being offered these tax breaks, reflecting that other factors such as improving the investment climate could be more effective in attracting investment.

On the contrary, some empirical evidence suggests that the effectiveness of investment incentives in attracting inward FDI depends on several factors, including the design features of incentives, characteristics of the investor, the nature of the investment, and the local context. For instance, efficiency-seeking FDI, which aims to reduce costs by optimising production for the global market, tends to be more responsive to tax incentives compared to resource-seeking or market-seeking FDI (James, 2013[4]).

Regarding design features, ex-post evidence shows that expenditure-based tax incentives, like accelerated depreciation have proven effective in stimulating investment in OECD countries such as the United Kingdom and the United States (Maffini, Xing and Devereux, 2019[12]; Zwick and Mahon, 2017[13]). Similarly, studies have found that expenditure-based tax incentives for research and development (R&D) can effectively induce investment in OECD countries. For example, in the United Kingdom, R&D spending among eligible companies increased by an average of 33% in response to tax incentives implemented in 2008 (Guceri and Liu, 2019[14]). Sungur (2019[15]) demonstrated that Türkiye's New Investment Incentive System, implemented in 2012 to promote investment in less developed regions through various schemes and support measures, successfully increased investment in those areas.

Another stream of literature has shown that the effectiveness of investment incentives can vary depending on local context. For example, accelerated tax incentives, like depreciation of capital expenditures in Poland, have produced mixed results. During periods of stability, Guceri and Albinowski (2021[16]) findings demonstrate that companies in Poland responded strongly with a positive investment response, while during a period of high uncertainty incentives did not prove very effective in stimulating investment for enterprises facing difficulties. Other authors have assessed that concurrent incentives of different types can have varying effects on FDI inflows. For instance, research by Bobenič Hintošová, Sudzina and

Barlašová (2021[17]) found that financial incentives had a positive and statistically significant direct effect on FDI inflows in the Slovak Republic between 2002 and 2019. Tax incentives had a statistically significant negative impact on inward FDI during the same period, however.

Additionally, empirical studies of investment incentives often struggle to accurately assess their impact, potentially overestimating or underestimating their effects. Some of the empirical work assessing investment incentives' effectiveness face challenges in isolating the precise effect of incentives amidst concurrent reforms aimed at enhancing the business environment. Countries often pursue growth-related reforms through a blend of approaches, including macroeconomic policies, improvements to the investment climate, and changes in industrial policies (Tuomi, 2012[6]).

The prevalence of investment incentives in OECD countries may be influenced by the fierce competition for FDI putting MNEs in a stronger position to request and negotiate incentives and the pressure felt by IPAs to secure investment projects in their jurisdictions. In this context, the OECD is seeking to enhance the design, governance, evaluation, and monitoring of incentives to maximise their benefits, providing policymakers and investment promotion practitioners with evidence-based guidance and tools to improve the effectiveness of these policies (Box 1.2).

Box 1.2. OECD ongoing work on investment incentives

The OECD's multi-year work programme on investment tax incentives is co-ordinated by the Investment Division and the Centre for Tax Policy and Administration's Tax Policy and Statistics Division. It aims to improve the understanding of challenges and opportunities that investment tax incentives pose for advancing sustainable development. The programme focuses on enhancing the design, governance, evaluation, and monitoring of incentives to maximise their benefits and encourage reform of wasteful incentives. It also examines the impact of the Global Minimum Tax (GMT) on tax incentive policies and investment promotion strategies.

The first phase of the programme included developing the OECD Investment Tax Incentives Database, which covers detailed information on the design and governance of tax incentives across 70 developing countries. Additionally, the programme extended the OECD's corporate effective tax rates (ETRs) model to create comparable indicators of tax incentive generosity and conducted country- and regional-level assessments on incentive use and policy goals.

Phase 2 will provide a practical guide to tax incentive policymaking in low- and middle-income countries and will focus on further implementing the OECD Council Recommendation on FDI Qualities for Sustainable Development, adopted in June 2022. This recommendation encourages prioritising sustainable development objectives when providing financial and technical support to stimulate investment. It calls for assessing how financial and technical support can address market failures failures hampering sustainable development and thereby help attract sustainable investment and improve firm capabilities, job quality, and workforce skills. Moreover, it stresses the importance of transparency and regular reviews of financial and technical support.

Sources: Celani, Dressler and Wermelinger (2022[2]), "Building an Investment Tax Incentives database: Methodology and initial findings for 36 developing countries", *OECD Working Papers on International Investment*, No. 2022/01, OECD Publishing, Paris, https://doi.org/10.1787/62e075a9-en; OECD (2022[11]); OECD Investment Tax Incentives Database – 2022 Update: Tax incentives for sustainable development" (brochure), OECD, Paris, www.oecd.org/investment/investment-policy/oecdinvestment-tax-incentives-database-2022-update-brochure.pdf; Celani, Dressler and Hanappi (2022[18]), "Assessing tax relief from targeted investment tax incentives through corporate effective tax rates: Methodology and initial findings for seven Sub-Saharan African countries", *OECD Taxation Working Papers*, No. 58, OECD Publishing, Paris, https://doi.org/10.1787/3eaddf88-en; OECD (2022[19]), "Recommendation of the Council on Foreign Direct Investment Qualities for Sustainable Development", *OECD Legal Instruments*, OECD/LEGAL/0476, OECD, Paris, https://legalinstruments.oecd.org/en/instruments/OECD-LEGAL-0476.

1.2. Objectives, types and legal framework of investment incentives

1.2.1. Investment incentives serve as a versatile tool for achieving diverse policy goals

FDI can play a crucial role in making progress towards the achievement of the Sustainable Development Goals (SDGs). By operating in host economies, foreign firms contribute to multiple SDGs through various channels (OECD, 2022[20]). These include fostering innovation through linkages with local firms, creating quality jobs, developing human capital, and deploying sustainable technologies to address climate change. Foreign firms can also play a pivotal role in promoting gender equality through inclusive workplace practices. Similarly, FDI attraction can help advance efforts to address climate change, particularly by attracting environmentally friendly industries and technologies (Aust, Morais and Pinto, 2020[21]).Foreign firms can also generate broader economic benefits beyond their direct operations. By interacting with local businesses, competing in the market, and exchanging workers, they can spur innovation, job growth, and better environmental and labour practices (OECD, 2022[20]).

Given the potential of FDI to contribute to economic, social and environmental objectives, investment incentives are often designed to align with these broader policy goals. The OECD survey findings indicate a strong focus on enhancing productivity and innovation, particularly in line with SDGs 8 (economic growth) and 9 (industry and innovation), with 74% of countries prioritising this policy goal when designing investment incentives (Figure 1.1). Additionally, employment creation and regional development are key objectives for almost half of countries, consistent with established evidence on the potential of FDI spillovers to reduce inequalities within countries and improve job quality (Echandi, Krajcovicova and Qiang, 2015[22]; OECD, 2022[20]). Survey results indicate that incentives are designed without specific policy goals beyond facilitating investment in the majority of countries (57%).

While productivity, innovation, employment and job creation remain core objectives behind the design of investment incentives across OECD countries, other SDG areas seem to be less critical. As such, less than a third of OECD countries use incentives to support climate change objectives according to IPAs. Digital transformation is even less prominent, with only 17% of countries using incentives to support it, despite the potential for FDI to deploy new technologies that advance decarbonisation and digitalisation (OECD, 2022[20]). Gender equality, social inclusion, and export promotion are not considered as primary objectives behind investment incentives. Although supporting the green and digital transitions are not reported as top policy objectives, many OECD countries do still offer a range of incentives to attract FDI for sectors that can support these goals, such as renewables, battery plants, electric vehicles and semiconductors (see section 1.4). This may reflect the fact that these sector-specific incentives aim rather at achieving broader economic goals, including productivity growth and job creation, rather than climate and digitalisation objectives.

Figure 1.1. Investment incentives in OECD countries typically aim to enhance productivity and innovation, but also target specific goals such as regional development and job creation

Top three policy objectives behind investment incentives (as reported by IPAs)

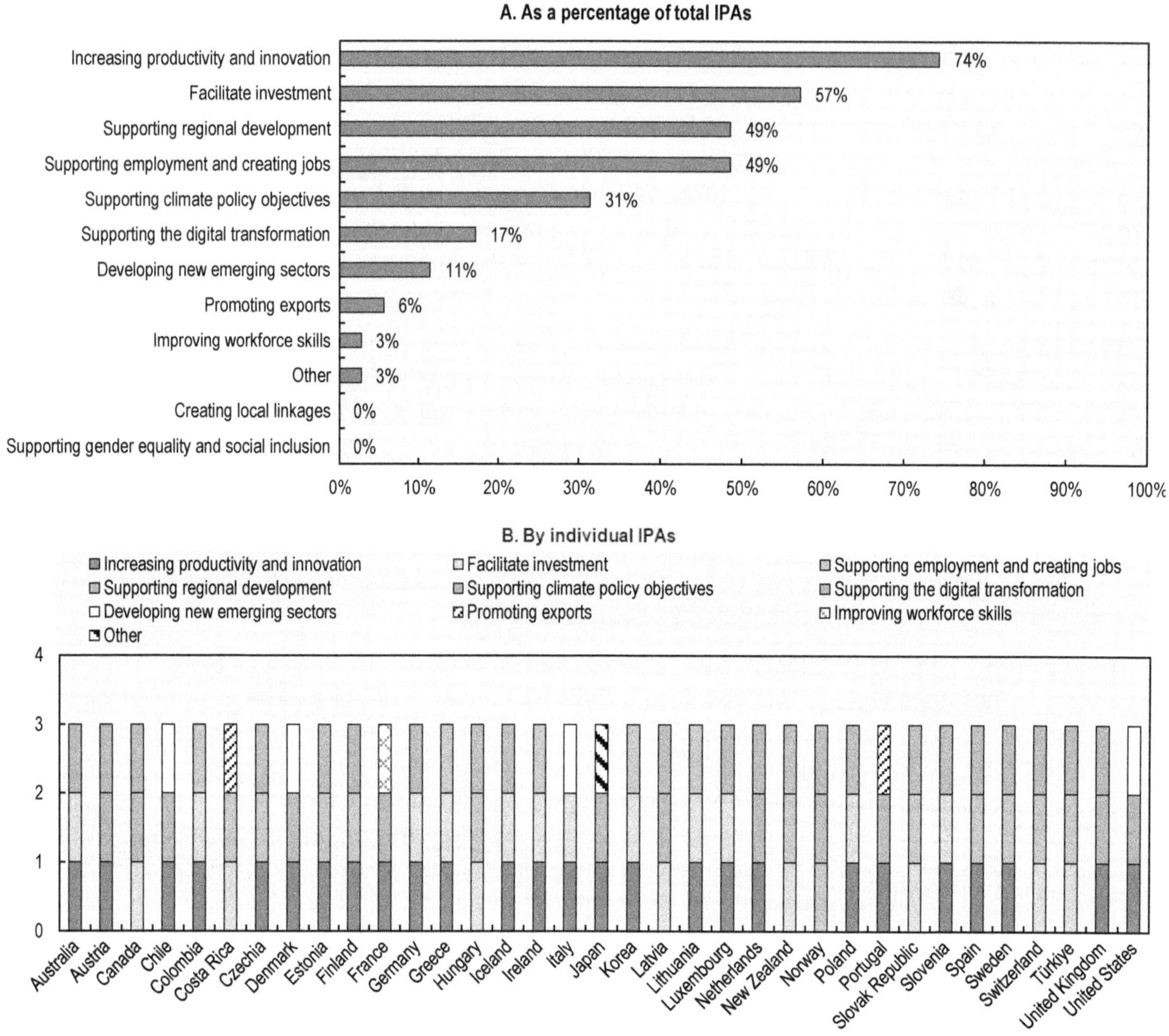

Source: OECD Survey on Investment Promotion and Investment Incentives, 2024.

1.2.2. Tax incentives are the most common type of investment incentive, surpassing non-tax incentives in terms of prevalence

According to surveyed IPAs, tax incentives are the most frequently used type of incentive across OECD countries, with 97% offering them, with Luxembourg being the exception. Financial incentives, such as direct loans and grants, are also widely utilised, with 86% of countries providing them, although they remain secondary to tax incentives. Regulatory and in-kind incentives, such as the provision of land or infrastructure, are less common in OECD countries, employed by 49% and 31% of countries, respectively. While tax incentives dominate the landscape, survey results confirm that all OECD countries implement more than one type of incentive, underscoring the complementary or even overlapping nature of financial, regulatory, and in-kind tools alongside tax incentives (Table 1.2).

Table 1.2. Investment incentives offered across OECD countries

OECD economies with at least one investment incentive, by type (as reported by IPAs)

	Tax Incentives						Financial incentives		In-kind benefits	Regulatory Incentives			Other non-tax incentives
Country	CIT	Social security contributions	Taxes on pay-roll	Taxes on property	Taxes on goods & services	Other tax incentives	Direct grants	Loans & guarantees	Provision of land & infrastructure	Differential regulation & standards	Specialised administrative assistance & services	Preferential treatment in public procurement	
AUS	■		■				■	■	■				
AUT	■					■	■	■					
CAN	■		■	■	■		■	■	■	■	■		
CHE	■							■					
CHL	■								■				
COL	■	■	■		■			■					■
CRI	■	■		■	■						■		■
CZE	■						■		■				
DNK	■	■					■	■					
ESP	■	■					■	■		■			
EST	■				■		■	■					
FIN	■						■	■			■		
FRA	■	■	■	■			■	■	■		■		
GBR	■						■				■		
GER		■					■	■			■		
GRC	■			■			■	■			■		■
HUN	■								■		■		
IRL	■		■	■	■	■	■	■					
ISL	■								■				
ITA	■	■					■	■			■		
JPN	■		■	■			■	■		■	■		
KOR			■	■	■				■				
LTU	■			■			■	■		■	■		
LUX							■	■	■				
LVA	■			■		■	■	■	■	■	■		
NLD	■	■	■				■	■					
NOR	■	■					■	■		■			
NZL						■	■			■			■
POL	■		■	■			■	■			■		
PRT	■	■		■			■	■			■		
SVK	■						■		■				
SVN	■						■	■					
SWE		■	■				■	■					
TUR	■	■		■	■	■	■	■	■	■	■	■	
USA	■						■	■					

Note: Coloured cells indicate the presence of at least one incentive of this type.
Source: OECD Survey on Investment Promotion and Investment Incentives, 2024.

Some OECD countries offer less conventional types of incentives to attract investments into specific sectors and locations. These include financial incentives such as direct equity investment and social security contribution incentives, as well as non-financial support like incubation programmes, employment assistance and streamlined administrative procedures. Examples of the latter include Korea's "red carpet" service for foreign investors and the Active Investor Plus Visa programme offered by New Zealand.

According to survey results, a significant majority (86%) of OECD jurisdictions use CIT incentives to reduce the tax burden on corporate profits, aiming to stimulate business activity (Figure 1.2.A). In countries using CIT incentives, expenditure-based incentives (tax credits and allowances)[1] are more commonly employed than income-based incentives (reduced rates and exemptions), with 60% using tax credits and 51% using tax allowances (Figure 1.2.B). Expenditure-based incentives are often considered by experts as more effective than exemptions because they more effectively target marginal investment projects as they are tied to investment expenditures, ensure benefits reach qualifying entities, and provide clearer tracking of incentive usage (Dama, Rota-Graziosi and Sawadogo, 2024[23]) (IMF, OECD, UN, World Bank, 2015[24]).

Figure 1.2. Within tax incentives, OECD countries predominantly grant CIT incentives, particularly expenditure-based incentives credits and allowances

Share of countries with at least one tax incentive (as reported by IPAs)

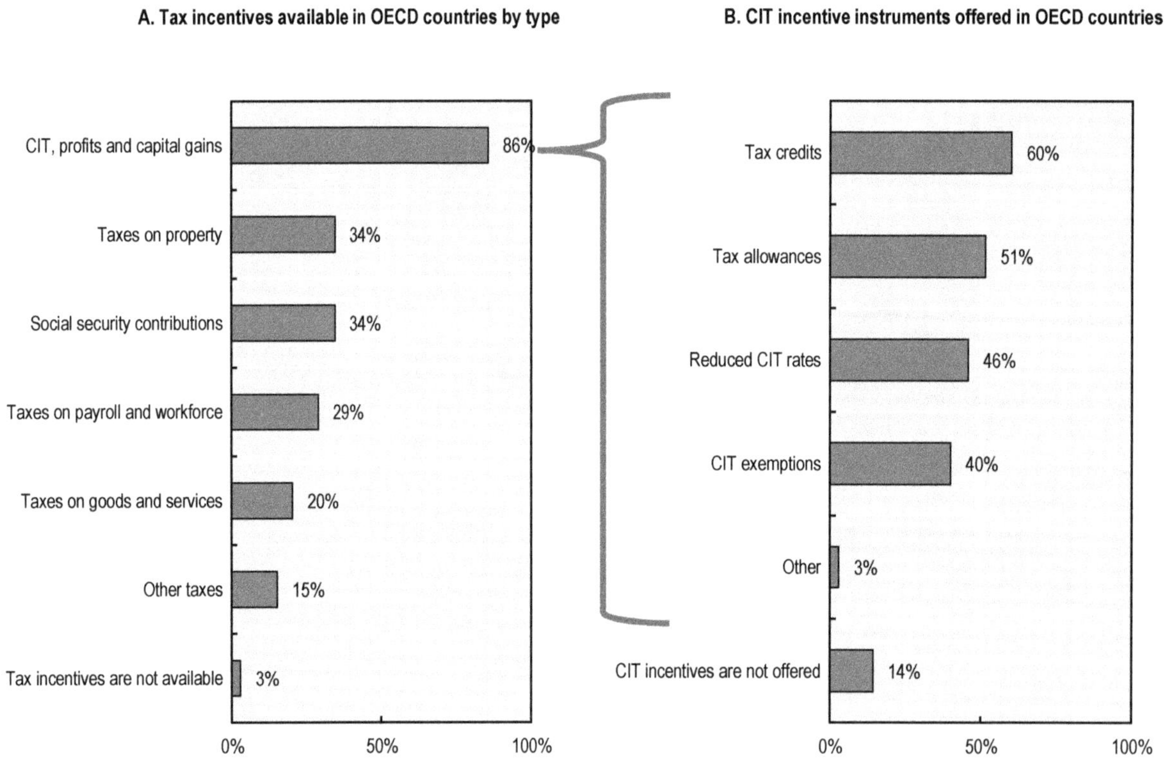

Source: OECD Survey on Investment Promotion and Investment Incentives, 2024.

Besides the strong preference for CIT incentives, OECD countries also tend to favour incentives for direct taxes over indirect taxes. According to respondents, incentives for property taxes and those for social security contributions are available in 35% of OECD jurisdictions, in both cases (Figure 1.2.A). Lowering property taxes can potentially stimulate investment in real estate development and infrastructure projects, particularly for greenfield FDI. Meanwhile, incentives on social security contributions can influence investment decisions, especially in labour-intensive sectors (Zhang, Chen and Song, 2022[25]; Kobayashi and Daigo, 2016[26]). Less than a third of respondents (29%) mentioned the availability of incentives for payroll taxes in their jurisdictions and 21% noted the existence of incentives for taxes on goods and services that can reduce the costs of investors' input.

Non-tax incentives, particularly direct grants, as well as loans and guarantees, are prominently deployed in the OECD, with approximately three out of four countries surveyed using them (Figure 1.3). Consistent with literature findings, financial incentives can play a significant role, especially in developed countries. Governments adopt financial incentives to support firms that may face credit constraints, hindering their ability to undertake investments even when profitable (Johnson and Toledano, 2022[27]). Financial incentives can also be particularly effective in attracting greenfield projects in countries with robust institutions, whereas tax incentives are more effective in countries with weaker institutional frameworks (Cuervo-Cazurra, Silva-Rêgo and Figueira, 2022[28]).

Figure 1.3. Financial incentives dominate the non-tax investment incentive spectrum

Share of countries with at least one non-tax incentive (as reported by IPAs)

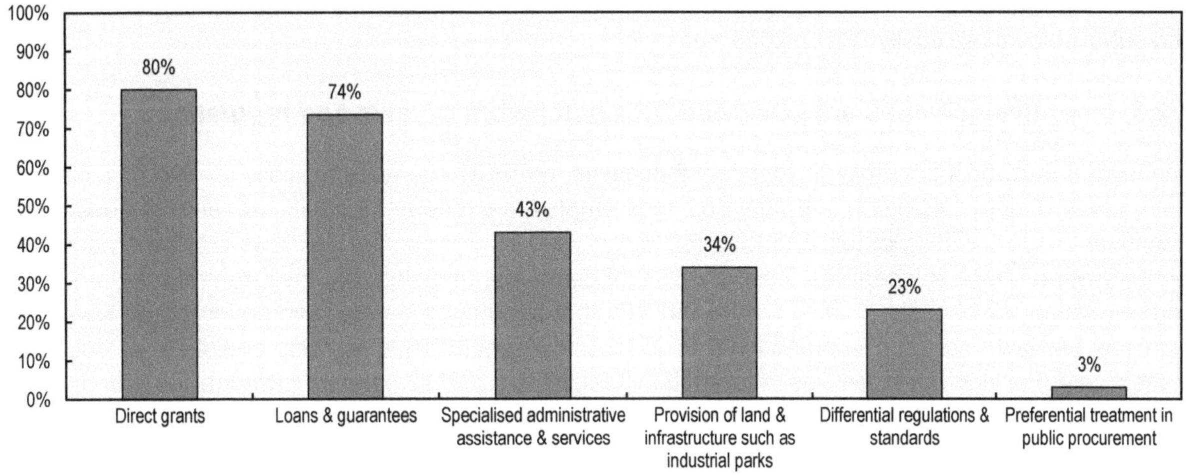

Source: OECD Survey on Investment Promotion and Investment Incentives, 2024.

In countries with strong institutions, stability and lower risks make direct financial support (like grants) more appealing, as investors can plan confidently. Conversely, in weaker institutional settings, tax incentives become crucial, as they may help offset higher risks and potential costs, improving long-term profitability and making investments more viable (Cuervo-Cazurra, Silva-Rêgo and Figueira, 2022[28]). The literature suggests also that the preference for financial incentives, such as direct grants, over tax incentives can depend on the type of activity and the investor. For instance, R&D grants might be more suitable for investors involved in fundamental or applied research, while R&D tax incentives typically encourage experimental development (OECD, 2020[29]). Financial incentives can also be particularly beneficial for investors in loss positions or those facing financing constraints, as they provide immediate support rather than deferred benefits (Hintošová and Barlašová, 2021[30]).

A variety of non-financial incentives are also offered by governments, though to a lesser extent compared to financial ones such as grants and loans. Specialised administrative assistance and services are used by 43% of OECD countries as reported by IPAs. This can be particularly helpful to facilitate investment, as OECD research finds that in 60% of OECD countries, investors need to engage with more than three public entities to establish a company (OECD, 2024[31]). Similarly, 34% of respondents reported that their jurisdictions provide land and infrastructure, such as industrial parks, to encourage firms to settle and develop in specific locations. Conversely, differential regulations and standards are less common, according to survey results, with just 23% of OECD governments offering them. The limited adoption of regulatory incentives aligns with economic literature, suggesting that countries with higher income levels typically boast better regulatory environments, diminishing the need for regulatory competition (FitzGerald, 2002[32]). According to the survey results, Türkiye's preferential treatment in public procurement can encourage greater investor participation in tenders. These incentives complement other measures, such as the introduction of an e-tendering system, which allows both domestic and foreign companies to register and submit bids more easily (WTO, 2023[33]).

1.2.3. Incentive schemes are governed by a patchwork of laws and regulations

The legal frameworks governing investment incentives in OECD countries typically involve multiple legal instruments (Figure 1.4.A). On average, countries employ five different legal instruments to govern their incentives mix, consisting of tax, financial, regulatory, and other benefits. Tax laws are the predominant legal framework for tax incentives, used by 86% of countries, underscoring their central role in defining and regulating tax benefits. Survey results indicate that tax incentives are also governed by laws other than the tax law, including supranational laws and investment laws, in 59% and 49% of countries, respectively. For non-tax incentives, supranational legislation and investment laws are the primary legal frameworks, used in 54% and 49% of cases, respectively, according to IPAs. Subnational regulations and sector-specific laws also wield a certain influence, particularly for non-tax incentives with 37% and 34%, respectively, highlighting the role of regional authorities and industry-specific regulations in shaping incentives for investors. While private negotiations with investors are used in granting both tax and non-tax incentives, these practices are relatively uncommon, occurring in only 14% and 20% of countries, respectively. Discretionary decisions in the provision of both tax and non-tax incentives can increase the risk of undue influence (IMF, OECD, UN, World Bank, 2015[24]).

Figure 1.4. Legal frameworks and information accessibility for investment incentives tend to be scattered

As a percentage of OECD countries (as reported by IPAs)

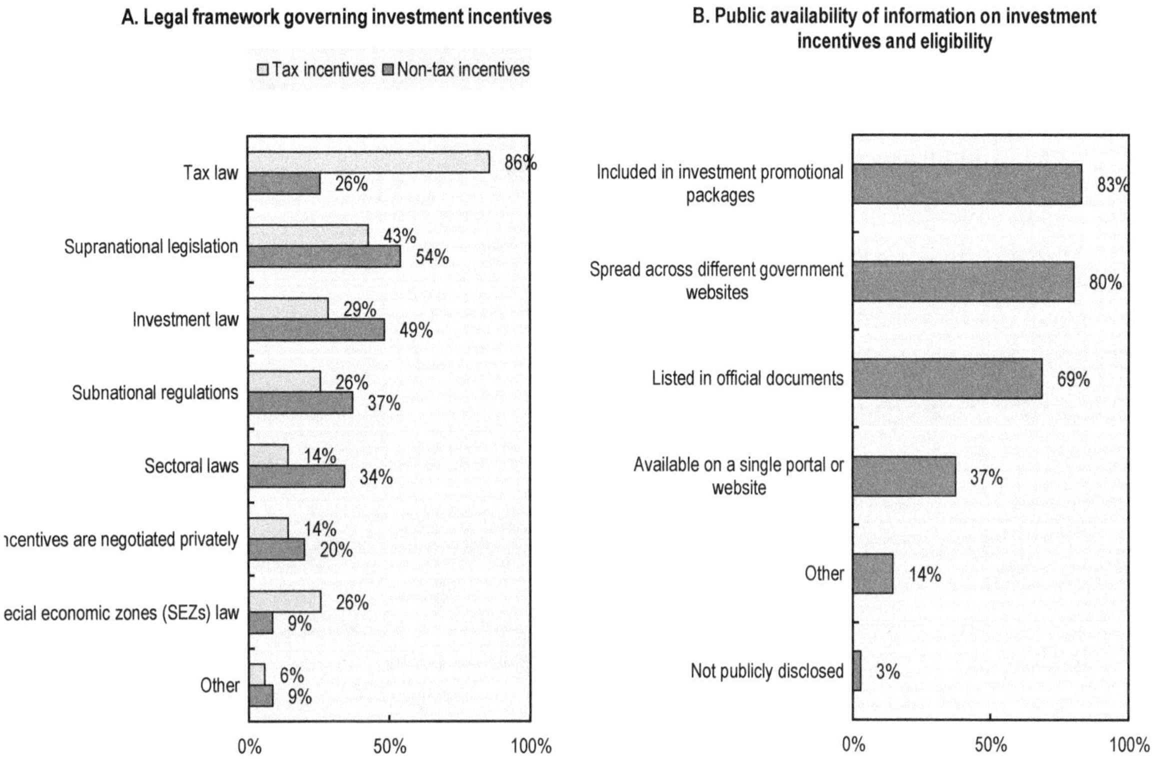

Source: OECD Survey on Investment Promotion and Investment Incentives, 2024.

Despite the multiple legal frameworks governing investment incentives in OECD countries, the majority of OECD IPAs (80%) report extensive awareness of the full spectrum of incentives available in their jurisdiction, with the remaining 20% demonstrating moderate awareness. From the investors' perspective, navigating scattered and complex legal frameworks can be time-consuming and limit their awareness of the full incentive regime. Incentives aimed at attracting investors prove ineffective if investors are unaware of them, or inefficient if they are only advertised to a limited audience (OECD, 2023[3]). While information on investment incentives and their eligibility is available in various forms, centralised platforms or websites dedicated to investment incentives are offered in only 37% of OECD jurisdictions according to respondents (Figure 1.4.B). For 80% of OECD countries, information on investment incentives and eligibility is typically scattered across various government websites. While an additional 83% also offer information in promotional materials (investor guides, B2B brochures, site visits), these materials can be difficult for potential investors to locate.

This dispersed structure across multiple regulations and multiple websites creates limitations in transparency of incentives for investment facilitation purposes. In many countries, transparency on incentives is limited by the fact that provisions governing incentives are spread out across numerous laws and regulations. Opaqueness on investment incentives may not only affect their potential uptake but also complicates assessments of their costs and benefits (OECD, 2023[3]). This points to the need for better co-ordination with other agencies for enhancing availability, accessibility and clarity of the information on investment incentives for investors (Box 1.3).

Box 1.3. Improving transparency of incentives for investment facilitation

In the context of the OECD's programme of work on investment incentives, the OECD aims to support enhanced transparency of investment incentives. The lack of a clear definition and typology for investment incentives has hindered governments' ability to assess transparency gaps and implement improvement measures. The OECD has set out key principles and a first set of guiding questions that can be part of a checklist to follow by policymakers to improve transparency of investment incentives.

Typology of investment incentives for enhanced transparency

The OECD has developed a comprehensive typology of investment incentives with three overarching types of investment incentives – i) tax, ii) financial and in-kind, and iii) regulatory and non-financial incentives, that are further sub-categorised by the specific instruments used to deliver investment incentives (e.g. for tax incentives the length of tax exemptions, the degree of CIT reductions, and the rate and applicability of tax allowances and credit).

Key principles for transparency

The OECD has established three core principles that can serve as a practical checklist for policymakers seeking to enhance transparency in investment incentives:

- **Availability:** Ensuring the comprehensive and up-to-date availability of all relevant information and legislation pertaining to investment incentives.
- **Accessibility**: Providing access to relevant legislation is particularly important given that incentive details are often not consolidated into one legal piece.
- **Clarity:** The information should be presented with clarity. While some incentive programmes may be inherently complex, the information provided should be readily understandable, minimising confusion for investors.

Source: OECD (2023[3]), "Improving transparency of incentives for investment facilitation", *OECD Business and Finance Policy Papers*, No. 35, OECD Publishing, Paris, https://doi.org/10.1787/ab40a2f1-en.

1.3. Design and scope of investment incentives

1.3.1. OECD countries often use stakeholder consultations and benchmarking in the design of investment incentives

The design of investment incentives is a crucial factor in determining their benefits and costs (OECD, 2024[34]) (OECD, Forthcoming[35]). Effective incentive design depends on various country-specific factors, including the type of industry, business size, and overall economic conditions (OECD, Forthcoming[35]). Factors like inflation and interest rates can also affect the cost and effectiveness of these programmes, highlighting the need for careful consideration during the design process. This involves selecting the appropriate type and instrument of the incentive, defining qualifying income or expenditures and other eligibility criteria, and determining the level of financial support. To determine these different factors, the design process involves consulting relevant stakeholders and, in some cases, considering the investment incentives offered by other countries.

Stakeholder consultations are integral to the design of investment incentives in OECD countries. While only three countries do not conduct consultations, 91% bring insights and perspectives from different actors, predominantly the private sector, as chambers of commerce and investors are consulted by 85% and 71% of countries, respectively (Figure 1.5.A). Engaging relevant parties, including the private sector, but also academia, trade unions and civil society, in inclusive decision-making processes helps building consensus on policy reforms related to investment and sustainable development (OECD, 2022[36]). Investment incentives with a legal basis often undergo a public consultation process as part of their development to gather input from various stakeholders. This approach facilitates the formulation of more effective policies and regulations and strengthens the legitimacy of decision making overall (OECD, 2020[37]).

The dialogue with the private sector can significantly inform the design of investment incentives, but the extent of this influence is moderate. According to the survey, private sector input has some influence in 53% of cases, but not necessarily a decisive role, as these inputs might be balanced with other factors such as observed market failures and policy objectives (Figure 1.5.B). For 19% of IPAs, private sector input plays a more limited role in shaping these programmes, which might be predetermined based on political priorities or when the incentives' governing legal framework is supranational legislation, as is often the case in EU countries. On the other hand, 16% of jurisdictions reported a more substantial private sector influence in shaping incentive programmes. This can be beneficial in identifying existing weaknesses, but it also raises concerns about the need to reflect the interests of society at large and avoid potential rent-seeking behaviour.

Figure 1.5. Business actors are highly consulted in the design of incentives

Consultation and involvement of stakeholders in incentive design as a percentage of OECD countries (as reported by IPAs)

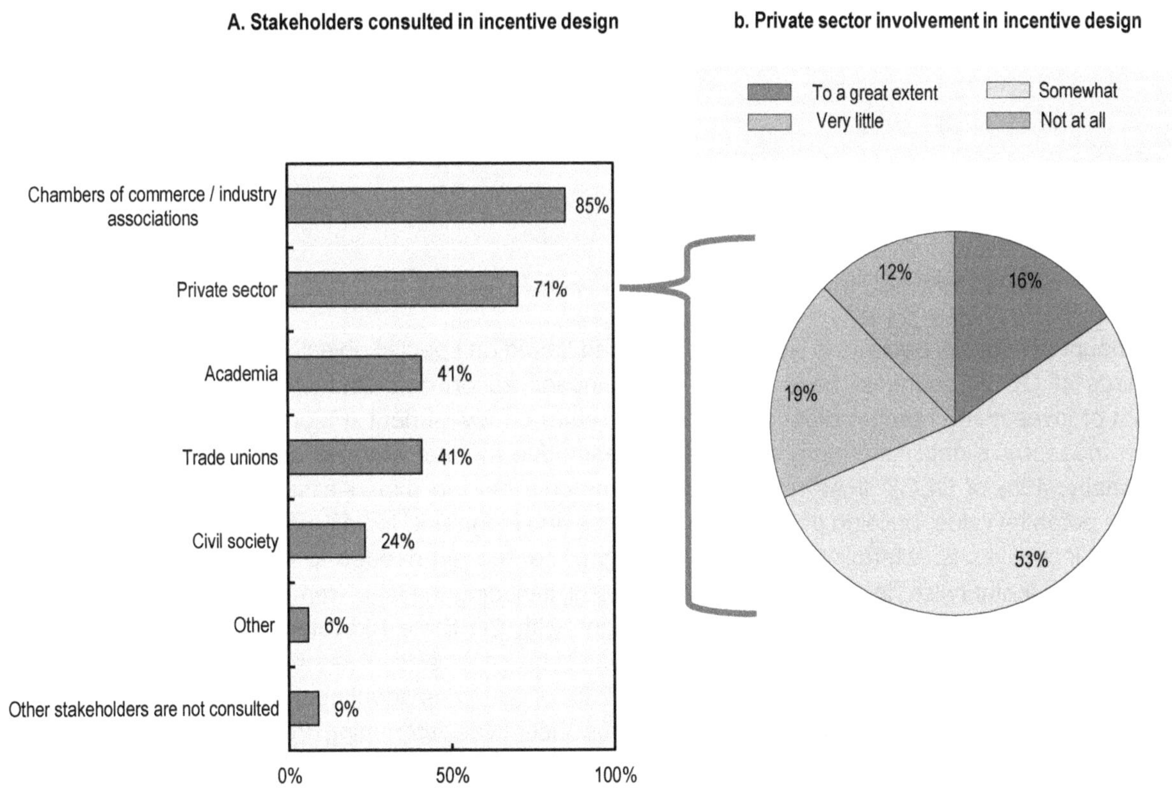

Source: OECD Survey on Investment Promotion and Investment Incentives, 2024.

According to IPAs, benchmarking other countries' incentive schemes is a common practice among OECD nations for designing incentives, with the vast majority indicating that it influences their approach in a way or another (Figure 1.6). While two-thirds of countries report considering other countries' incentives to some extent, only 12% use investment incentive decisions from other jurisdictions to a great extent, meaning they could replicate or overbid those offered by other countries. One out of five countries reports limited influence of international benchmarking in their design. There is a risk that overreliance on benchmarking may lead to incentives being designed merely to match those of other countries rather than responding to domestic needs, potentially resulting in inefficiencies (Tuomi, 2012[6]).

Figure 1.6. Benchmarking other countries' incentive schemes is a common practice in the OECD

As a percentage of OECD countries (as reported by IPAs)

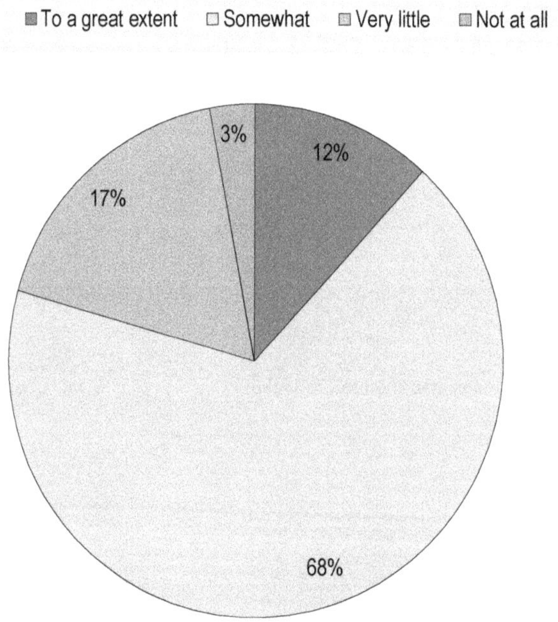

Source: OECD Survey on Investment Promotion and Investment Incentives, 2024.

The amount of financial benefits is typically determined based on specific objectives and parameters. Over two-thirds of OECD countries base their financial incentives on quantitative parameters, such as the amount of investment, number of jobs created and return on investment (Figure 1.7). These parameters rely on measurable data, offering greater transparency due to clear and pre-defined evaluation criteria. Additionally, 43% of OECD IPAs report that governments rely on expert assessments to estimate the project's potential value, building on data with expertise and judgment. In 34% of jurisdictions, the financial benefit of incentives is determined by the funding gap, i.e. the aid needed to attract an investment that would not occur otherwise. In another 34%, other criteria, including the legal framework, are used to assess the benefit. For EU OECD countries, this often aligns with EU State Aid rules, where the aid intensity (percentage) depends on geographic location and company size. Negotiating incentive amounts individually with investors is less common, with only 26% of countries adopting this approach. This method often involves significant pressure to offer generous incentives, stemming from internal lobbying and external competition from other countries offering attractive packages (OECD, 2023[38]; IMF, OECD, UN, World Bank, 2015[24]). Only three countries use benchmarking practices to estimate the amount of the benefit to be granted in their incentive packages with those of other countries. Such benchmarking may lead to over-subsidising projects and misallocating resources, potentially resulting in a 'bidding war' where countries focus on matching offers rather than addressing market failures or reducing project costs efficiently based on local conditions (Christiansen, Oman and Charlton, 2003[39]).

Figure 1.7. OECD countries often determine financial benefits using quantitative parameters and expert assessment

Criteria used for determining the financial benefit in incentive design (as reported by IPAs)

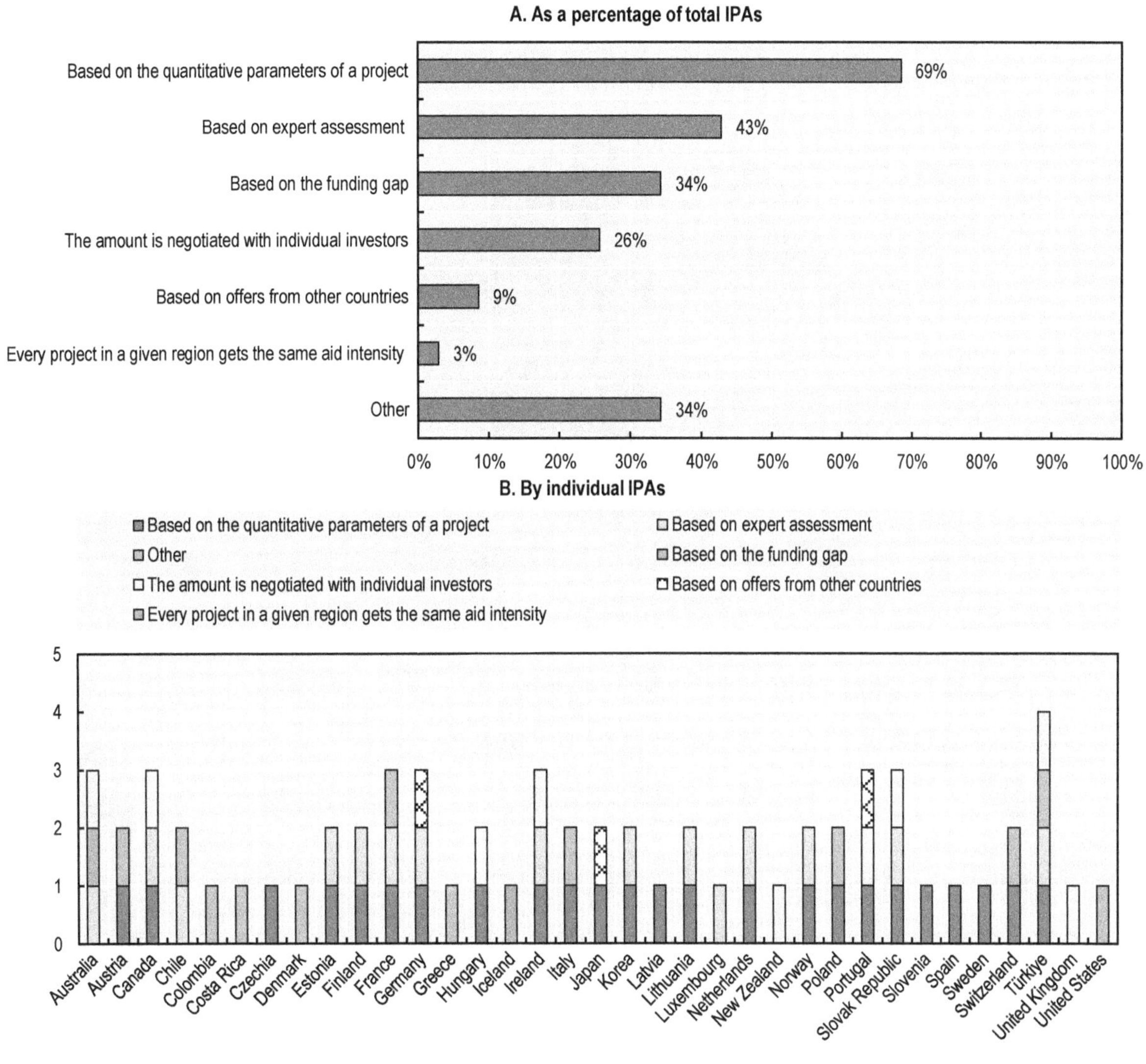

Source: OECD Survey on Investment Promotion and Investment Incentives, 2024.

1.3.2. Incentives often include investment size criteria; firm size, ownership or origin conditions are rare

Investment size conditions are typically used by policymakers in the design of incentives. According to IPA reports, most OECD countries (83%) have at least one incentive programme that includes investment size conditions, be it the minimum amount invested or the number of jobs created. Almost half use dual conditions based on both capitals invested and jobs created (Figure 1.8). The remaining programmes rely on either the investment amount alone (28%) or job creation solely (6%). Investment size conditions could ensure that resources are used efficiently while limiting incentives to large investments can also reduce administrative costs for the government (Celani, Dressler and Wermelinger, 2022[2]; IMF, OECD, UN, World Bank, 2015[24]). But setting a high investment threshold might exclude smaller businesses or innovative startups, or sectors that are not labour-intensive. For example, the Lithuanian parliament recently adjusted the Green Corridor for Large-Scale Investment Projects incentive by introducing a less stringent full-time job creation requirement. This change reflects an adaptation to the increasing capital intensity of manufacturing projects, aiming to attract more FDI in digital sectors (Box 1.4).

Figure 1.8. In most jurisdictions, investment incentives are contingent upon the size of the investment

Percentage of countries with investment size criteria for at least one incentive (as reported by IPAs)

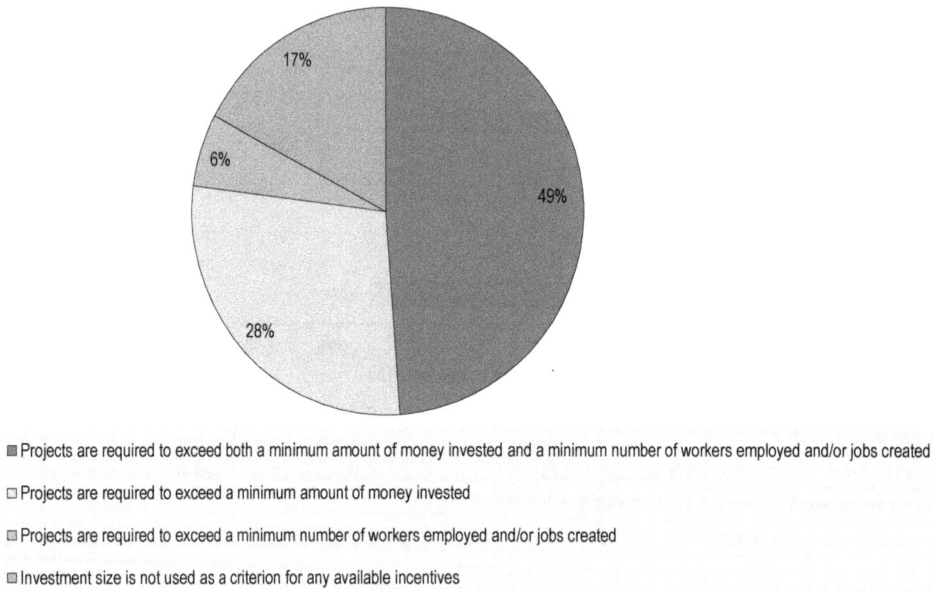

Source: OECD Survey on Investment Promotion and Investment Incentives, 2024.

Box 1.4. Green Corridor for Large-Scale Investment Projects Multiple target

The green corridor for large-scale investment incentive combines size, location, and sectoral criteria, offering benefits such as 0% CIT for up to 20 years, contingent on meeting specific performance requirements.

Recently, legislation introduced a change in the eligibility conditions. While the original criteria required investors to create at least 150 new full-time jobs (200 in Vilnius), the new rules allow companies to qualify by creating between 20 and 149 new jobs (or 20-199 in Vilnius), provided that at least 20 of these positions offer wages at or above 1.25 times the average municipal wage. This adjustment reflects a shift toward accommodating projects with higher capital intensity and less labour intensity.

Source: The Ministry of the Economy and Innovation of the Republic of Lithuania. Sector activities available at: https://eimin.lrv.lt/en/sector-activities/investment/.

While investment size conditions are common across OECD countries, they are generally unrestricted in terms of firm size or origin. The survey shows that in three-quarters of OECD jurisdictions, governments do not discriminate between foreign and domestic investors when granting incentives, or between large firms and small and medium-sized enterprises (SMEs) (Figure 1.9.A). While attracting investment from large and foreign enterprises is often seen as particularly valuable because it can provide access to capital and technology unavailable in the domestic market (Johnson and Toledano, 2022[27]), attracting SMEs is often overlooked. However, their smaller size can also be an advantage, providing greater flexibility to accelerate innovation and adopt new technologies (OECD, 2022[40]). Moreover, SMEs tend to rely more on local suppliers and partners compared to MNEs, increasing the potential for productivity and innovation spillovers to local economies (UNCTAD, 2024[41]; OECD, 2023[42]). They are also less likely to crowd out local firms, positioning them as potential game changers in a global context characterised by increased competition for a shrinking pool of large-scale projects. (UNCTAD, 2024[41]).

Figure 1.9. Investment incentives are generally unrestricted in terms of firm size, ownership or origin

Percentage of countries with firm-type conditions used as a criterion for at least one incentive (as reported by IPAs)

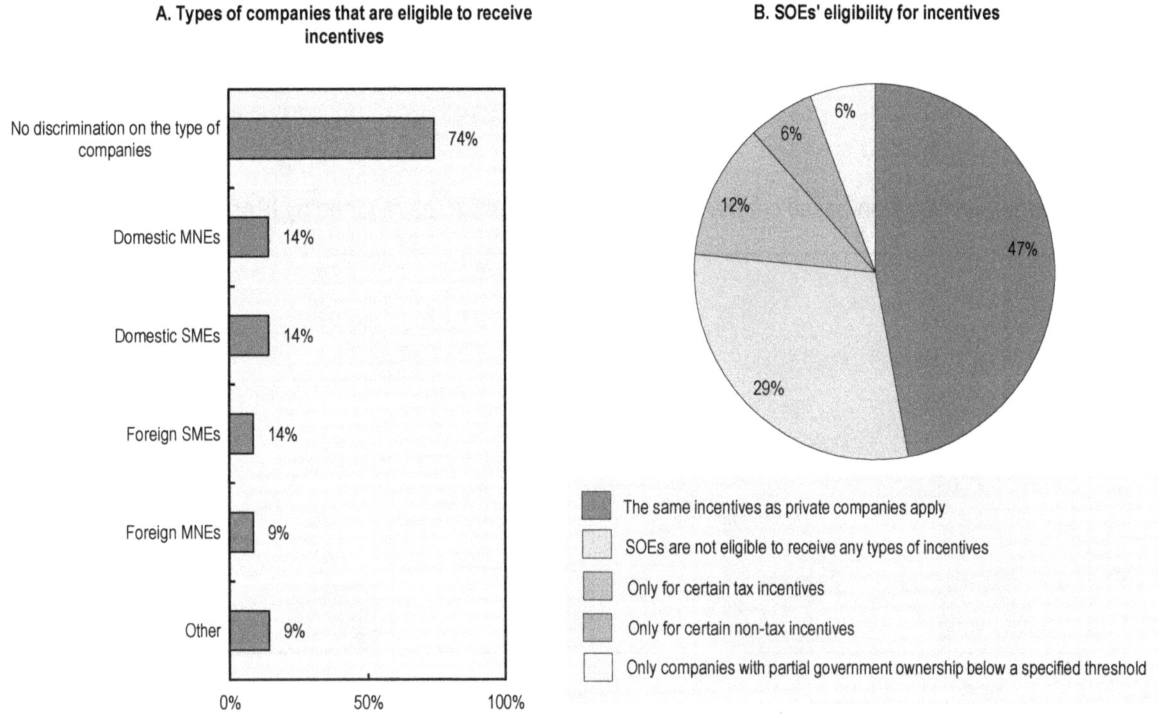

Source: OECD Survey on Investment Promotion and Investment Incentives, 2024.

Similar to the absence of discrimination based on firm size or origin, most OECD jurisdictions also allow state-owned enterprises (SOEs) to apply for investment incentives according to IPAs. Globally, SOEs account for 20% of investment, and foreign SOEs are increasingly interested in entering developed markets through international mergers (Huq et al., 2024[43]). According to survey results, 65% of OECD jurisdictions allow SOEs to apply for investment incentives and this share goes to 71% when including companies with limited government ownership (Figure 1.9.B). Nearly half provide SOEs with access to the full range of incentives available to private companies. In 12% of jurisdictions, SOEs receive specific tax incentives, while another 6% offer them non-tax incentives. The degree of government ownership can influence eligibility, however. For instance, Germany and Canada restrict access to incentives for fully owned SOEs, suggesting a stricter approach for businesses of the state. On the other hand, a significant portion of jurisdictions (29%) exclude SOEs from investment incentives. This exclusion can be attributed by concerns that SOEs receiving incentives could alter the playing field (OECD, 2012[44]).

1.4. Sector and location-based targeting of investment incentives

Location-based conditions are a prevalent feature of investment incentive design across OECD countries, with 32 out of 35 surveyed jurisdictions using them for at least one incentive. These conditions often target underdeveloped or remote areas specifically. Notably, two-thirds of IPAs report that location-based incentives are primarily targeting remote or less developed regions (Figure 1.10). This focus aligns with the broader policy goal of reducing regional disparities as showcased in section 1.2. Supporting evidence comes from the observation that, across the OECD, the top 10% of regions attract 700 times more FDI than the bottom 10% (OECD, 2022[45]). The emphasis on regional development is further underscored by the fact that 72% of OECD countries have dedicated regional investment promotion strategies, and 94% of national investment promotion strategies incorporate a regional development dimension (OECD, 2022[45]). To further concentrate investment, a third of IPAs indicate that at least one of their incentives targets investments within special economic zones (SEZs). In contrast, location-based criteria targeting industrial parks are less common, being present in less than a quarter of jurisdictions according to survey results.

Figure 1.10. Location-based conditions are frequently used in OECD incentives, often targeting remote or underdeveloped areas

Share of countries with location-based criteria for at least one incentive (as reported by IPAs)

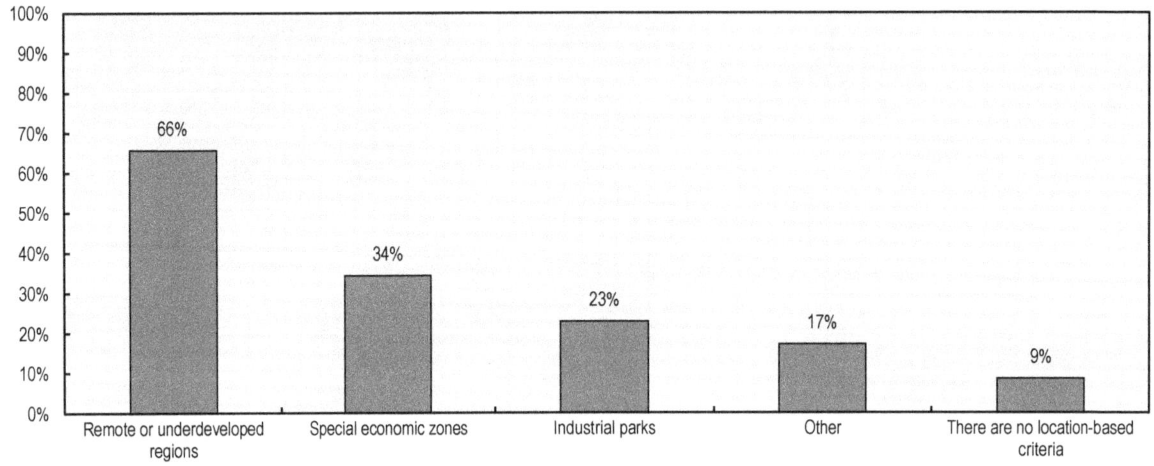

Source: OECD Survey on Investment Promotion and Investment Incentives, 2024.

Additionally, OECD countries commonly use sector-based conditions to grant investment incentives, as 77% use incentives specifically designed to target selected sectors. Sector targeting is sometimes used to contain the fiscal costs of tax incentives and to benefit only those projects, sectors, and sub-sectors that are considered most in need or likely to create social and economic spillovers (Celani, Dressler and Wermelinger, 2022[2]). It also carries the risk of misallocation of resources, however, such as directing incentives in sectors that would have attracted investment anyway.

OECD countries tend to target sectors that promote a more digital and environmentally sustainable economy, and this shift is reflected in the sectors that receive the most incentives. According to IPAs, 66% of OECD countries offer at least one incentive for the renewable energy sector, while 57% provide incentives for the battery and electric vehicle industry – sectors that are essential to the green transition. These two sectors are among the top three targeted sectors on a list of 30 possible options (Figure 1.11). Similarly, sectors crucial for the digital transformation, such as semiconductors (51%), information and communication technologies (49%), and artificial intelligence (40%), are among those with the highest reported prevalence of incentives, according to IPAs. Conversely, traditional sectors, such as forestry and wood, textile and clothing, real estate, oil and gas, and retail, receive much less incentives. This strategic focus is reflected in the substantial growth of climate focused FDI, which surged from less than 2% of global greenfield investment in 2005 to 39.4% in 2022 (fDi intelligence, 2023[46]).

Figure 1.11. Sector-based incentives target the green and digital transitions, aligning with OECD IPA priorities

Percentage of countries offering at least one incentive in a specific sector and of IPAs prioritising a specific sector (as reported by IPAs)

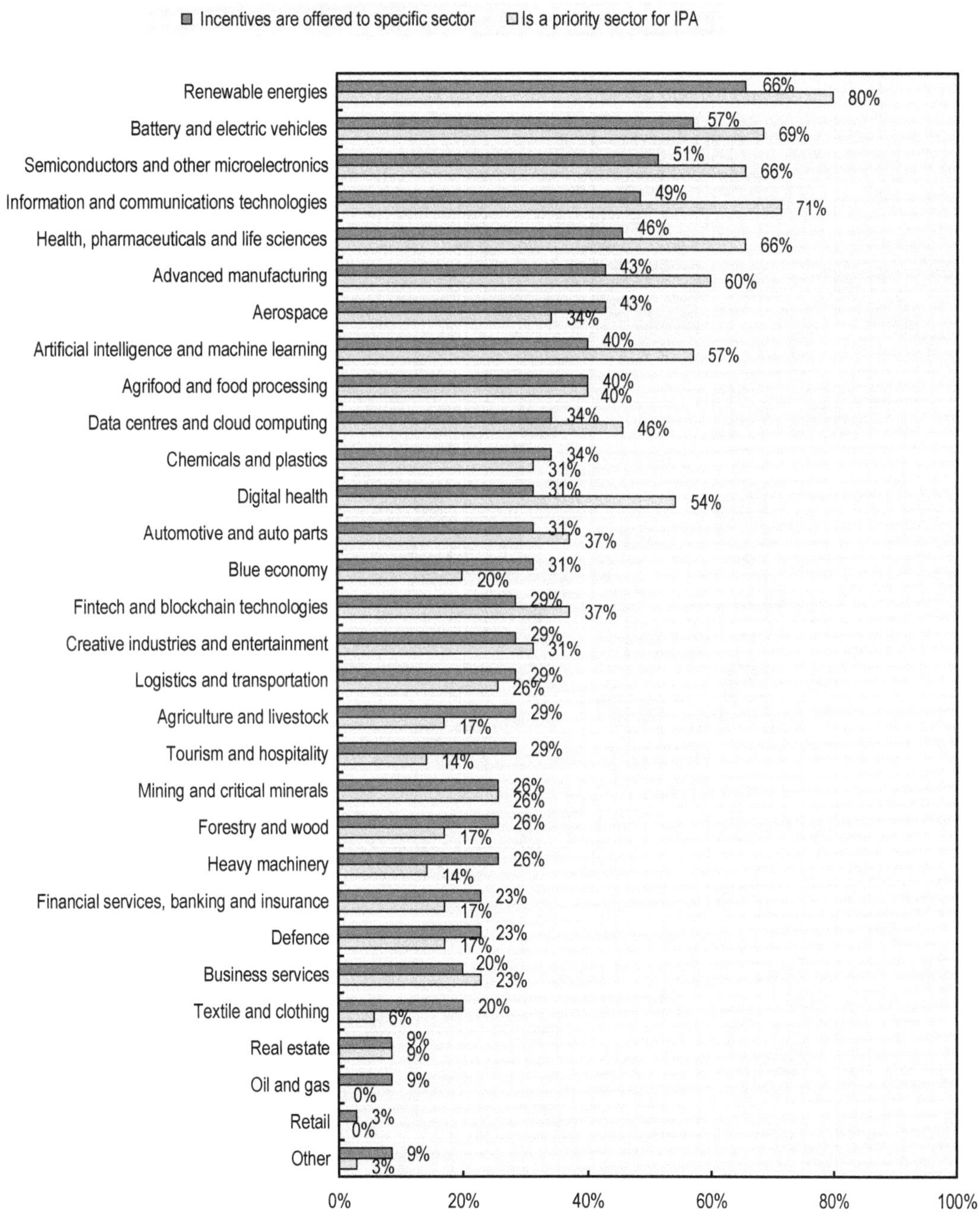

Source: OECD Survey on Investment Promotion and Investment Incentives, 2024.

Table 1.3. Sector-specific conditions in incentives and the prioritisation of sectors by IPAs are common practices among OECD countries.

Targeted sectoral incentives and IPA sectoral priorities, by country (as reported by IPAs)

Country	Advanced manufacturing	Aerospace	Agriculture and livestock	Agrifood and food processing	AI and machine learning	Automotive and auto parts	Battery electric vehicles	Blue economy	Business services	Chemicals and plastics	Creative industries and entertainment	Data centres and cloud computing	Defence	Digital health	Financial services (bank and insurance)	Fintech and blockchain technologies	Forestry and wood	Health, pharmaceuticals and life sciences	Heavy machinery	ICT	Logistics and transportation	Mining and critical minerals	Oil and gas	Real estate	Renewable energies	Retail	Semiconductors and microelectronics	Textile and clothing	Tourism and hospitality	Other
AUS	✓						✓															✓			✓					
AUT					✓									✓				✓		✓					✓		✓		✓	
CAN	✓	✓	✓	✓	✓	✓	✓	✓		✓	✓	✓	✓	✓	✓	✓	✓	✓	✓	✓	✓	✓	✓		✓		✓			
CHE																														
CHL				✓					✓		✓									✓					✓					
COL			✓	✓					✓		✓						✓								✓				✓	
CRI	✓	✓	✓	✓	✓	✓		✓	✓	✓	✓	✓		✓		✓		✓	✓	✓	✓						✓	✓	✓	
CZE		✓					✓											✓							✓		✓			
DNK			✓				✓		✓						✓										✓					
ESP	✓	✓	✓	✓	✓	✓	✓	✓		✓	✓	✓	✓	✓			✓	✓	✓	✓	✓				✓		✓	✓		
EST	✓			✓	✓	✓	✓			✓		✓	✓	✓	✓	✓	✓	✓		✓		✓			✓		✓			
FIN																														
FRA	✓	✓	✓	✓	✓		✓	✓			✓	✓	✓	✓		✓	✓	✓		✓		✓			✓		✓	✓	✓	✓
GBR																														
GER		✓			✓		✓													✓		✓			✓		✓			
GRC	✓		✓	✓	✓		✓	✓	✓	✓	✓	✓		✓	✓	✓		✓	✓	✓	✓			✓	✓		✓	✓	✓	
HUN																														
IRL																														
ISL							✓	✓													✓				✓				✓	
ITA	✓	✓		✓	✓	✓	✓	✓		✓	✓	✓		✓				✓	✓	✓	✓	✓		✓	✓		✓	✓	✓	
JPN	✓				✓		✓					✓		✓	✓	✓		✓		✓					✓		✓			
KOR	✓	✓					✓			✓	✓									✓					✓		✓			
LTU												✓	✓																	
LUX																														
LVA																														
NLD		✓		✓			✓	✓		✓				✓				✓		✓					✓		✓			
NOR			✓					✓										✓					✓		✓					
NZL																														
POL		✓			✓	✓	✓			✓					✓	✓		✓				✓			✓		✓			
PRT			✓	✓				✓									✓			✓	✓				✓				✓	
SVK	✓			✓	✓	✓	✓		✓	✓		✓	✓			✓		✓	✓	✓							✓	✓		
SVN	✓	✓		✓	✓	✓	✓					✓					✓	✓	✓	✓							✓		✓	
SWE	✓					✓	✓			✓							✓		✓		✓	✓			✓					✓
TUR	✓	✓				✓	✓						✓		✓	✓					✓				✓		✓			
USA	✓	✓	✓	✓	✓	✓	✓	✓	✓	✓	✓	✓	✓	✓	✓	✓	✓	✓	✓	✓	✓	✓	✓	✓	✓	✓	✓	✓	✓	

Note: ✓ = Incentives offered = Priority sector for IPA.
Source: OECD Survey on Investment Promotion and Investment Incentives, 2024.

Sector targeting is a common approach in OECD investment promotion, with IPAs often focusing on at least two specific industries (Table 1.3). As part of their investment promotion strategy, OECD IPAs prioritise some sectors by dedicating more resources to develop tailored tools to attract and support investment in these areas. The survey suggests that OECD IPAs tend to prioritise a wide range of sectors, with an average of ten per agency. The distribution shows that 26% of IPAs prioritise 0-5 sectors in their investment promotion strategies (Figure 1.12). A larger share, 37%, focuses on 6-11 sectors, while 29% targets 10-14 sectors. However, only 8% of IPAs prioritise more than 15 sectors. This indicates that while IPAs have a sectoral approach to their promotion strategies, their focus is typically on specific sectors rather than a broader, more general approach to all sectors. The literature suggests that IPAs are more likely to succeed when they focus strategically on promoting specific sectors. Existing research shows that sector targeting results in higher FDI inflows (Harding and Javorcik, 2012[9]). One study focusing on OECD countries found that IPAs targeting industries increased FDI inflows into those industries by 41% (Charlton and Davis, 2007[47]). Having many priority sectors, even though could be less distortive, it could result in spreading budget and human resources across numerous sectors, leading to a lack of expertise and focus. IPAs may struggle to develop tailored strategies and marketing materials, as well as outreach efforts for each sector when dealing with such a broad range of industries.

Figure 1.12. OECD IPAs typically focus on multiple sectors for investment promotion

As a percentage of OECD IPAs

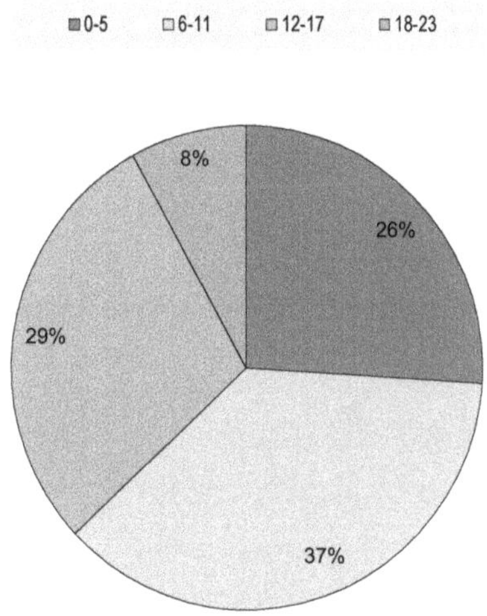

Source: OECD Survey on Investment Promotion and Investment Incentives, 2024.

Note

[1] Tax allowances may relate to current expenditure (e.g. operation expenses) or capital expenditures. Tax allowances may allow for a faster write-off of the value of capital expenditure from taxable income up to 100% of incurred costs (i.e. acceleration) or can go beyond 100% of acquisition cost (i.e. enhancement). This could include, for example, allowing firms to deduct 150% of the value of a new machine. Tax allowances for current expenditure are always enhancing. Source: OECD (2022[1]) "Investment Tax Incentives Database – 2022 Update: Tax incentives for sustainable development (brochure)", OECD Publishing, Paris, https://www.oecd.org/investment/investment-policy/oecd-investment-tax-incentives-database2022-update-brochure.pdf.

2 The role of incentives in promoting investment: Strategic importance for IPAs and institutional implications

This chapter builds on data from the 2024 *OECD Survey on Investment Promotion and Investment Incentives* to highlight the importance of investment incentives in the broader investment promotion strategies of IPAs and discusses how they perceive and use incentives to attract various types of FDI projects. The chapter also examines the role of national IPAs in the governance of incentive design and management, including their role in the promotion of incentives, the efficiency of co-ordination mechanisms as well as their involvement in monitoring and evaluating their use and impact.

2.1. Investment incentives within IPAs' investment promotion strategies

2.1.1. Investment incentives often align with IPAs' overall priorities, but there's a lack of consistent incentive support for some sectors

Investment incentives are generally aligned with the strategic objectives and priority sectors of IPAs in most OECD countries (Figure 2.1). The survey reveals that 94% of participating IPAs report a certain degree of alignment between the incentives granted in their country and at least one of their tools or priorities – be it their strategic objectives, priority sectors, key performance indicators (KPIs), priority projects or priority investors. Only Denmark and Switzerland report no alignment between their incentive regime and their IPA priorities. While incentives are typically designed by ministries or other agencies, 83% of IPAs consider that they align with their strategic goals, making them instrumental in achieving these objectives. Additionally, 71% of IPAs report that incentives match their target sectors, thus helping to focus their investment promotion efforts on government-designated priority industries, such as digital and green sectors (Section 1.4). Just over a half of IPAs indicate that incentives are aligned with their priority projects, which are defined by specific characteristics like potential for high innovation, significant job creation, or substantial capital investment.

Figure 2.1. OECD incentive schemes often align with the strategic objectives and priority sectors of IPAs

Alignment of Incentives (as reported by IPAs)

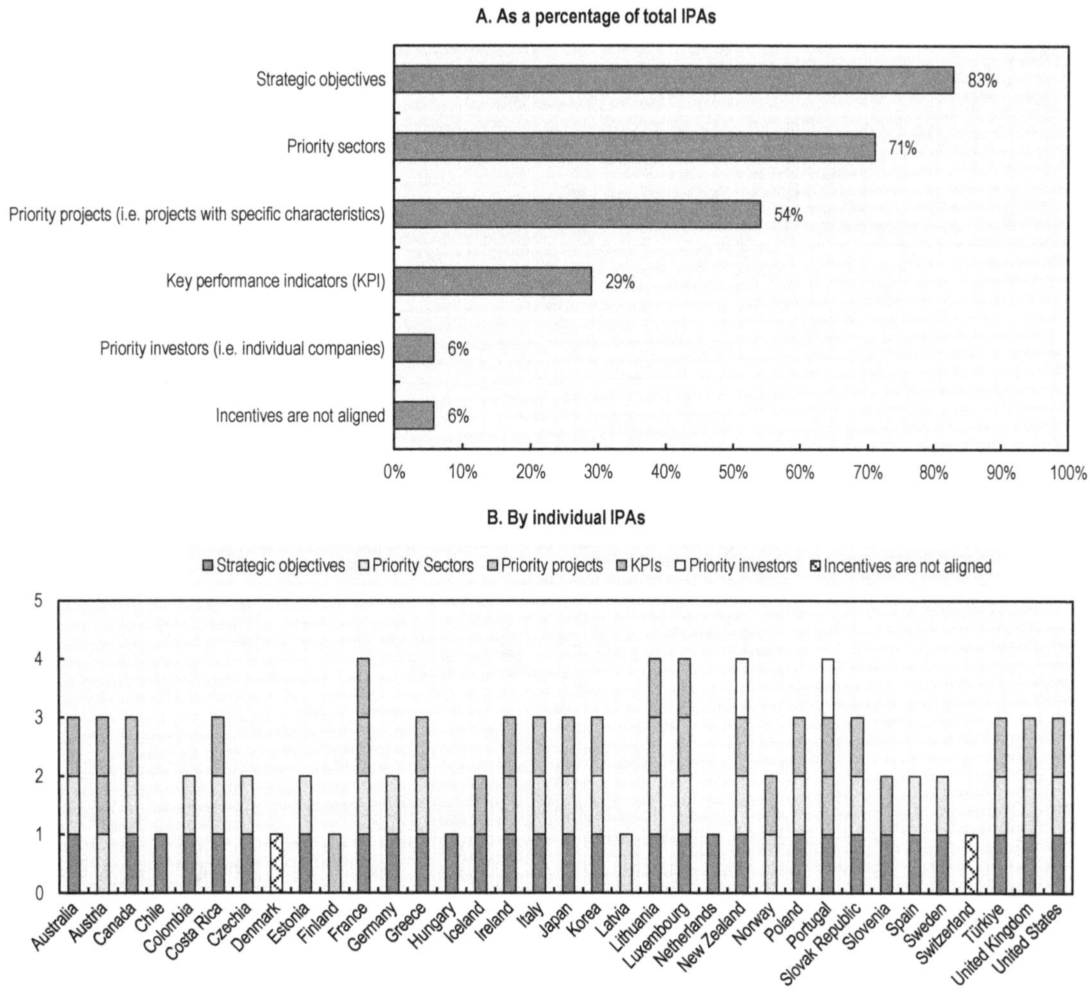

Source: OECD Survey on Investment Promotion and Investment Incentives, 2024.

While a majority of IPAs report that incentives are aligned with their priority sectors, the survey reveals a slight misalignment between the sectors targeted for investment incentives and those prioritised by IPAs (Figure 2.2). There are 13 sectors (43% of all possible sectors) that are considered a priority by IPAs but where incentives are not always provided, particularly in high value-added sectors like advanced manufacturing, renewable energies, digital health, health and pharmaceuticals, and ICT. Conversely, 14 sectors (47%) see a higher portion of countries offering incentives than those prioritised by IPAs. These include textile and clothing, tourism and hospitality, and heavy machinery. There is a perfect match between the sectors targeted by investment incentives and those prioritised by IPAs in only 10% of the assessed sectors, notably mining and critical minerals, agrifood and food processing, and real estate. To address this, improved co-ordination between investment policymakers involved in designing and targeting sectors and IPAs, which are at the forefront of investment promotion, is crucial.

Figure 2.2. Limited overlap between sector-specific incentives and IPA prioritised sectors highlights need for better co-ordination

Percentage gap between average OECD sector-specific incentives and IPA-identified priority sectors

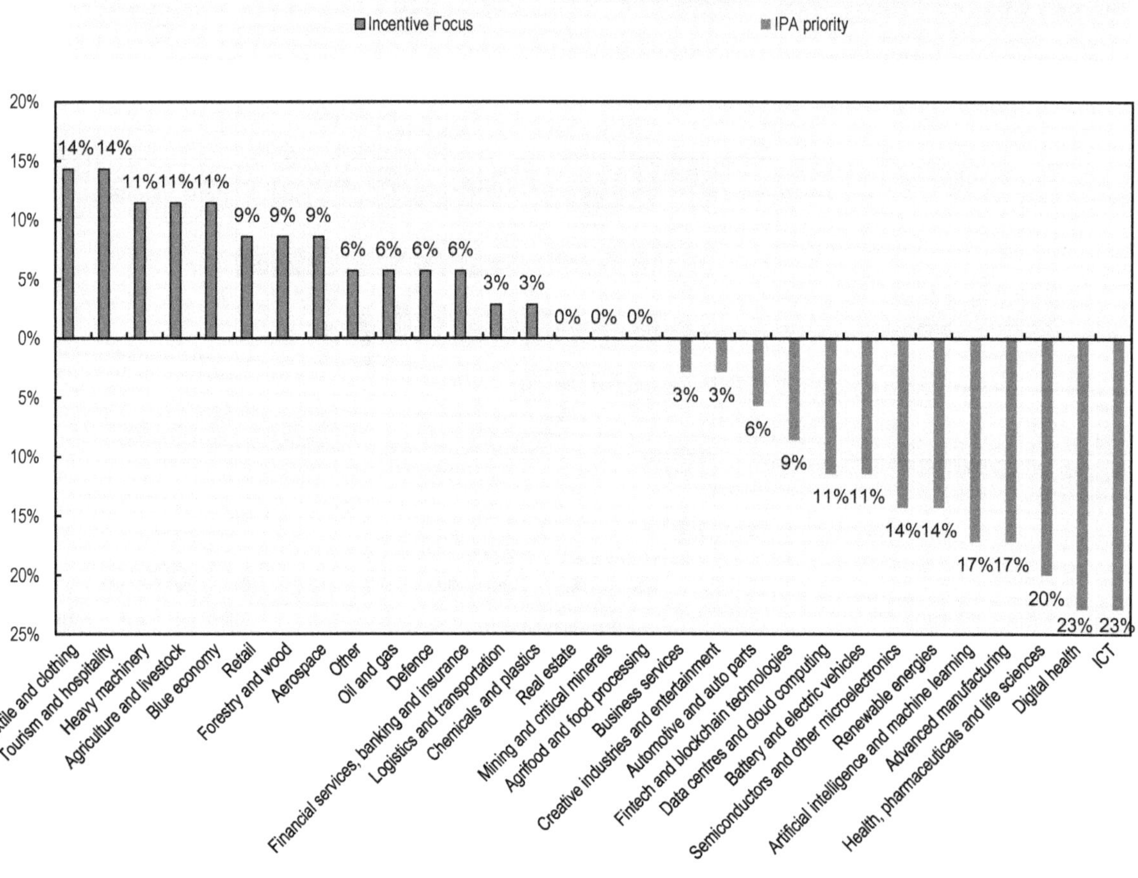

Note: Sectors labelled as "Incentive Focus" have a higher percentage of countries offering incentives compared to the percentage of IPAs that consider the sector a strategic priority. The difference between these percentages is shown on the graph. Conversely, sectors labelled as "IPA Priority" have a higher percentage of IPAs prioritising the sector compared to the percentage of countries offering incentives. The difference is also shown on the graph.
Source: OECD Survey on Investment Promotion and Investment Incentives, 2024.

2.1.2. OECD IPAs typically consider investment incentives as one of several factors influencing investment decisions

The investment location decisions of MNEs are influenced by a host of factors that are context-driven with important spatial and sectoral differences (OECD, 2023[48]). In this context, a significant portion of OECD IPAs do not consider incentives, particularly tax incentives, to play a critical role in foreign firms' location decisions (Table 2.1). On a scale from 0 to 10, CIT tax incentives are rated 5.3 by IPAs on average, indicating moderate relevance for MNE location decisions. Other tax incentives are even less influential with an average ranking of 4.7. Non-tax incentives receive a higher average ranking of 6.5, indicating they are perceived as somewhat important but not decisive factors. Only a small percentage of IPAs consider incentives to hold significant weight in location decisions, with 12% of IPAs giving a score of 9-10 for CIT tax incentives, 6% for other tax incentives, and 24% for non-tax incentives. Scholars echo this view, noting that tax incentives rarely drive location choices, as firms first select locations that meet their basic production needs and then seek incentives (Katitas and Pandya, 2024[49]). Thus, incentives often serve as a tiebreaker during the final stages of negotiations between investors and governments of shortlisted investment locations (Andersen, Kett and von Uexkull, 2018[8]).

Table 2.1. IPAs tend to consider that incentives are not a deciding factor for investment location

(With 1 being the lowest and 10 the highest)

Class Interval of Scores	Providing/promoting CIT tax incentives	Providing/promoting other tax incentives	Providing/promoting non-tax incentives
0-2	15%	18%	3%
3-5	36%	48%	36%
6-8	36%	27%	36%
9-10	12%	6%	24%
OECD average	5.3	4.7	6.5
OECD G20 average	4.4	4.7	6.6
OECD non-G20	5.7	4.7	6.4

Source: OECD Survey on Investment Promotion and Investment Incentives, 2024.

When comparing perceptions across OECD IPAs, smaller economies – particularly non-G20 countries – place relatively higher importance on CIT incentives for MNE location decisions. In contrast, larger countries tend to place more weight to non-tax incentives. Additionally, the correlation between a country's GDP size and the emphasis on incentives shows that IPAs from smaller economies consider incentives more critical in investment location decisions (Figure 2.3). Similarly, from a geographic perspective, IPAs from OECD Latin American countries rate incentives as more significant than those in other regions, with scores of 6.7 for CIT incentives, 7.0 for tax incentives, and 7.7 for non-tax incentives, all above the OECD average.

Figure 2.3. IPAs from smaller economies tend to place greater importance on incentives in investment location decisions

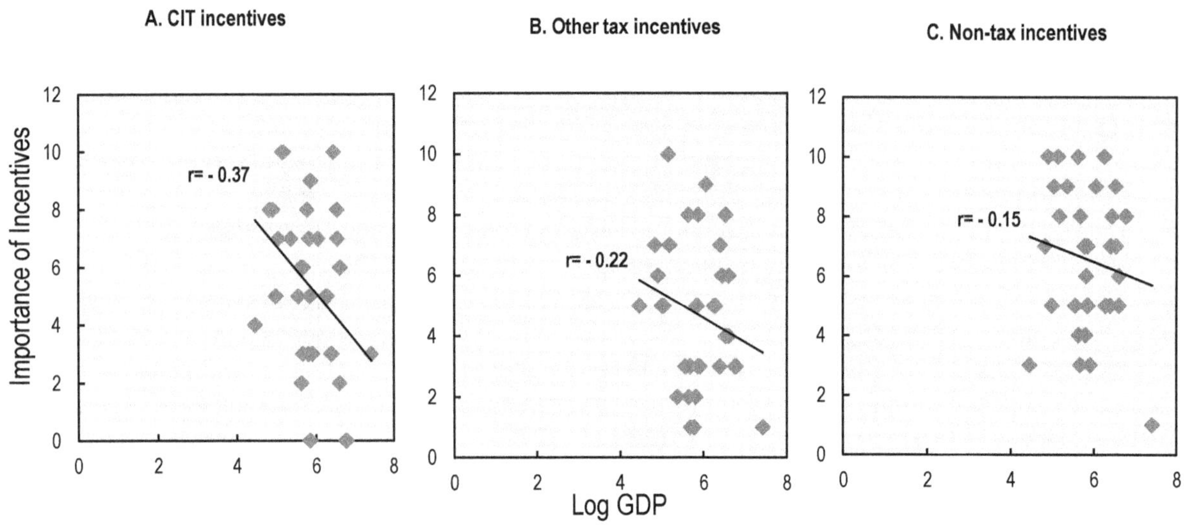

Source: OECD Survey on Investment Promotion and Investment Incentives, 2024.

Alongside these findings, incentives are often considered lower-ranking factors compared to other factors that are important to attract FDI, regardless of the type of investment (Table 2.2). Factors like the quality of infrastructure and connectivity, the availability of an educated workforce, and an enabling legal and administrative environment are the top factors across the three main types of investments, whether natural resource-seeking, export oriented or market-seeking. The size of market and growth prospects is the perceived as the most important factor for the latter. When looking at incentives more carefully, it is for export-oriented investments, which aim to exploit cost advantages in production for global markets, that CIT incentives rank the highest as compared to other incentives, yet only at the 7th place when compared to other factors. In contrast, for natural resource-seeking investments, which aim to exploit local resources, and market-seeking investments, which focus on penetrating a local market, CIT incentives are even less important, at the 8th and 9th positions, respectively.

The survey findings coincides with recent literature highlighting that investors typically do not prioritise incentives highly among the factors influencing their investment decisions (Johnson and Toledano, 2022[27]) In contrast, factors such as the availability of skilled workforce, market size and growth prospects, robust infrastructure, and an enabling legal and administrative environment are typically ranked higher. Natural resource availability is understandably crucial for natural resource-based investments, but less so for export-oriented and domestic-market projects. This result also aligns with research that highlights essential factors MNEs consider when choosing investment locations. These factors include governance reforms, development of local suppliers, investments in domestic hard and soft infrastructure, human capital, and upholding the rule of law, characterised by predictability, transparency, credibility, accountability, and fairness (OECD, 2015[50]; Danzman and Slaski, 2021[5])

The slight variations in rankings across investment types highlight the relative importance of different incentives. CIT incentives tend to hold a stronger position compared to other tax incentives, particularly for export-oriented investments. This could be because exporting firms are typically highly mobile and cost-oriented, seeking to reduce expenses for products destined for the global market (Lewis and Whyte, 2022[51]). Conversely, investors oriented toward domestic markets are less sensitive to tax incentives, finding financial, in-kind and regulatory incentives more relevant.

Table 2.2. IPAs tend to rank the provision of incentives lower than other factors in attracting firms across different types of investments

By average ranking (from most important to least important factor)

Rank	Natural Resources Investments	Export-Oriented Investments	Domestic market-oriented investments
1st	Existence of natural resources	Good infrastructure or connectivity	Size of market and growth prospects
2nd	Good infrastructure or connectivity	Availability of an educated workforce	Availability of an educated workforce
3rd	Availability of an educated workforce	Size of market and growth prospects	Good infrastructure or connectivity
4th	Enabling legal and administrative environment	Enabling legal and administrative environment	Enabling legal and administrative environment
5th	Size of market and growth prospects	Availability of suppliers	Availability of suppliers
6th	Good R&D capabilities and infrastructure	Good R&D capabilities and infrastructure	Good R&D capabilities and infrastructure
7th	Low business costs	**Provision of CIT incentives**	Low business costs
8th	**Provision of CIT incentives**	**Provision of non-tax incentives**	**Provision of non-tax incentives**
9th	Availability of suppliers	**Provision of other tax incentives**	**Provision of CIT incentives**
10th	**Provision of non-tax incentives**	Low business costs	**Provision of other tax incentives**
11th	**Provision of other tax incentives**	Existence of natural resources	Existence of natural resources
12th	Other	Other	Other

Note: Not all IPAs provided rankings for all investment types. This could be due to a lack of relevant projects in certain sectors (e.g., natural resources) within some countries.
Source: OECD Survey on Investment Promotion and Investment Incentives, 2024.

Some IPA professionals may perceive investment incentives as effective tools for investment attraction, particularly those with limited prior experience in the private sector and in developing countries IPAs where employee performance is often evaluated based on closed deals (Danzman and Slaski, 2021[5]). Findings in this report show, however, that IPA professionals do not consider investment incentives are decisive factors as compared to other criteria. Investment incentives, while important, are not perceived as the primary driver of investment attraction by OECD IPAs. Instead, IPAs use a multifaceted approach to attract FDI, where the promotion of investment incentives constitutes one component of their overall strategy. To attract and facilitate FDI, IPAs use a combination of functions, including image-building, investment generation, investment facilitation and retention, and policy advocacy (OECD, 2018[52]). When compared to key activities within these functions, OECD IPAs view the provision and promotion of tax and non-tax investment incentives as the least important elements of their strategies (Table 2.3). In contrast, measures related to image-building, investment facilitation and investment generation are ranked first, second and third, suggesting that delivering core activities and services to attract investment is considered more important than offering investment incentives.

Table 2.3. Incentives are relatively less important compared to other measures undertaken by OECD IPAs in their promotion strategies

Average ranking out of 10 possible options (from most important to least important measure)

Measures For Investment Promotion	Average Ranking
Marketing the country as an attractive investment destination	2.1
Providing services during the establishment phase	3.2
Conducting investment generation on targeted sectors, industries and projects	3.3
Advocating for a friendlier business environment	5.2
Providing aftercare services	5.3
Organising and attending public relation events	6.1
Providing/promoting CIT tax incentives	6.4
Providing/promoting non-tax incentives	6.7
Providing/promoting other tax incentives	7.1
Other	9.7

Source: OECD Survey on Investment Promotion and Investment Incentives, 2024.

IPAs hence recognise that their strategies must go beyond investment incentives to effectively influence investors' behaviour. Agencies are actively shaping investment promotion strategies through innovative initiatives. To attract the attention of global investors, some IPAs are crafting compelling country brands that effectively communicate unique value propositions, highlighting competitive advantages and showcasing the investment climate. Others are providing comprehensive support, from initial market research and site selection to business setup, support for talent identification and ongoing aftercare services (Box 2.1).

Box 2.1. Beyond incentives: Innovative measures for to promote investment in selected OECD countries

Choose France Summit

Choose France aims to present and explain to major international companies the existing investment and reforms being carried out to promote economic activity in France. It also highlights the importance of international investment in supporting growth, innovation and employment throughout France.

Every year, almost 400 bilateral meetings are organised between the President of the Republic, ministers, and the heads of foreign and French companies to discuss their plans for setting up in France. According to the French Government, the results of Choose France Summit are the following:

- 10 451 foreign investment projects in France over the period 2017 to 2023.
- 307 940 jobs maintained or created between 2017 and 2023.
- France remains the most attractive country for foreign investment for the fifth year running.

Invest Japan Hotline

JETRO's hotline aims to facilitate investor setup by offering consultations regarding the administrative procedures required for FDI into Japan. Besides arranging meetings with officials of regulatory agencies if needed, a JETRO staff member will escort the foreign company or foreign-affiliated company representative and provide language support during the consultation with the relevant authorities.

The hotline can also be used to improve the business climate, as investors can request regulatory reforms. After examining the request, the Cabinet Office will ask the relevant authorities to consider possibilities of reform. Certain answers from the relevant authorities may be reported to the Regulatory Reform Council for discussion. The result of the deliberation at the Council will be reported to the foreign company or foreign-affiliated company through JETRO if it is to be released to the public.

Source: Elysée (2024[53]), "Choose France", https://www.elysee.fr/emmanuel-macron/choose-france; and JETRO (2024[54]), Invest Japan Hotline, https://www.jetro.go.jp/en/invest/jetros_support/hotline/.

2.1.3. The limited role of incentives in investment promotion suggests OECD IPAs will not shift strategies with the introduction of the Global Minimum Tax

The evolving global tax landscape, including the implementation of the Global Minimum Tax (GMT)[1] could affect the role of both tax and non-tax incentives in OECD IPAs' promotion strategies. The GMT mandates a 15% effective tax rate, in every jurisdiction where they operate, for large MNEs groups with annual global revenues exceeding 750 EUR million. This requirement may limit the effectiveness of certain tax incentives that reduce firms' ETRs below 15% (OECD, 2022[55]). Differences in taxation between jurisdictions are estimated to fall, which will likely increase the importance of non-tax factors in influencing investment decisions and could improve the allocation of capital globally (OECD, 2024[56]).

In this context, the majority IPAs in the OECD (60%) report that they do not expect a change in their investment promotion strategy (Figure 2.4). This reflects that the promotion strategies of OECD agencies are generally not overly relying on tax and non-tax incentives. Conversely, among those expecting to modify their strategies, a combination of different measures will be undertaken, with 29% of IPAs planning to streamline bureaucratic procedures, the same share focusing on improving regulatory certainty and the quality of legislation, and an equal percentage shifting to other types of tax and non-tax incentives. Only seven IPAs are expecting to focus more on strengthening their marketing efforts.

Figure 2.4. The GMT is not expected to prompt major changes in IPA promotion strategies

Expected changes of investment promotion due to the GMT (as reported by IPAs)

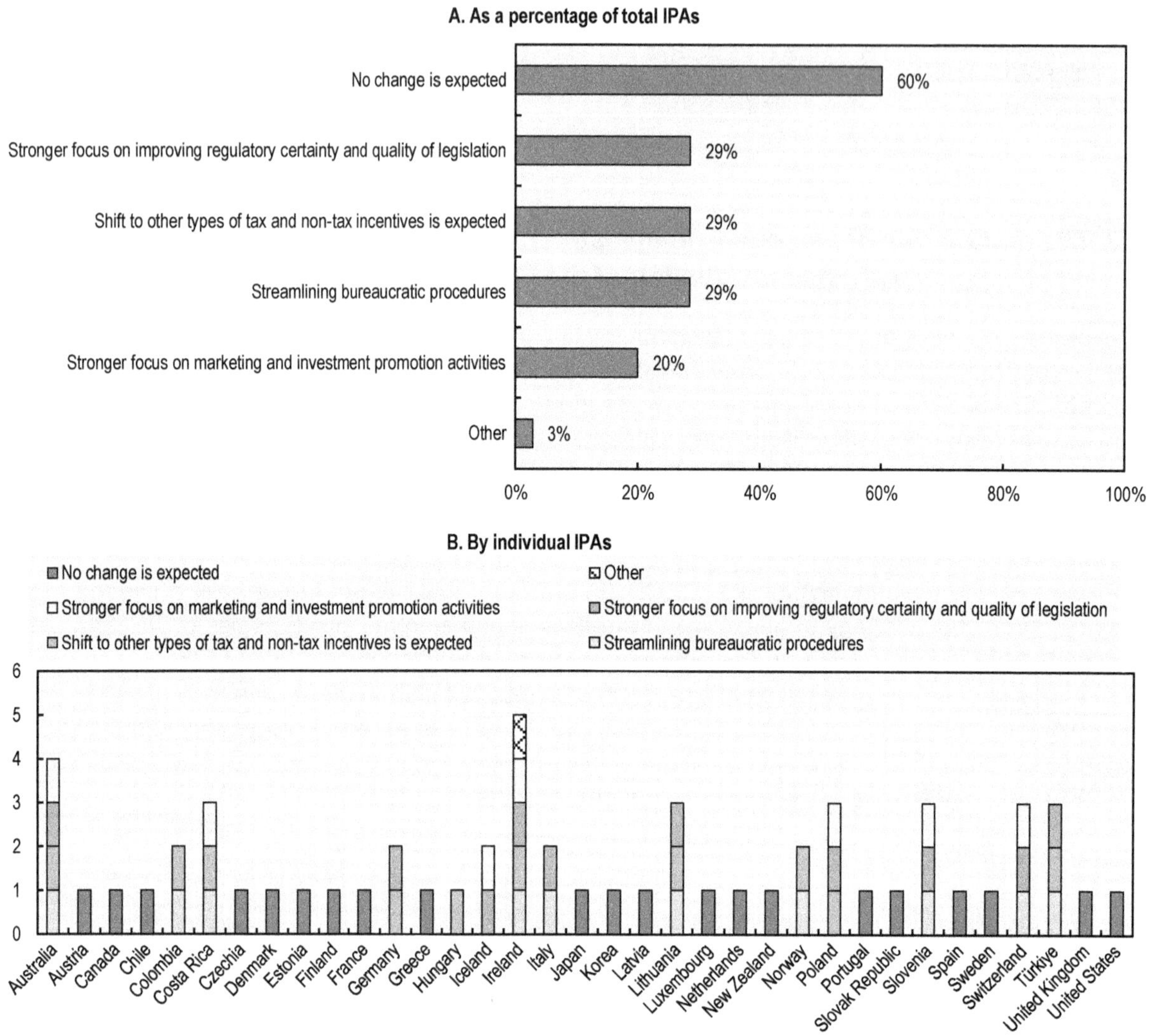

Source: OECD Survey on Investment Promotion and Investment Incentives, 2024.

2.2. The role of IPAs in the governance of investment incentives

The design, granting and monitoring of investment incentives involve a complex interplay among different institutions. This leads to diverse institutional governance arrangements, where the role of IPAs in providing, designing and evaluating incentives varies widely across OECD countries, especially since other national and subnational institutions are often involved. Similarly, the M&E of investment incentives for assessing their effectiveness also involve different institutional arrangements. The participation of multiple stakeholders results in various collaboration mechanisms.

2.2.1. IPAs mostly serve as the main focal point on incentives and can play a relatively more important role for non-tax incentives

IPAs can play different roles in the governance of tax and non-tax incentives, but, overall, the survey shows that IPAs are more active in the latter (Figure 2.5.A) For instance, Invitalia, the Estonian Investment Agency, Germany Trade & Invest, LuxInnovation, Spirit Slovenia, New Zealand Trade and Enterprise and the United Kingdom Department for Business and Trade, do not directly participate in the governance of tax incentives but actively participate in several functions related to non-tax incentives (Figure 2.5.B). This could be because CIT and other tax incentives tend to be governed mostly by tax laws, under the responsibility of tax authorities and finance ministries, while non-tax incentives typically involve a broader range of institutions depending on the types of incentives. The survey results show that OECD IPAs are operational agencies and mainly act as promoters of incentives, as they serve as contact points rather than being directly involved in designing or granting them. More than half of agencies (57%) serve as the main contact point for information on tax incentives while 69% do so for non-tax incentives. IPAs also play a significant role in advocating for incentives, with 40% doing so for tax incentives and 57% for non-tax incentives. In the same vein, IPAs are consulted much more often for the design of non-tax incentives (60%) than for tax incentives (37%). However, IPAs are less involved in directly designing and granting incentives. No OECD IPA has the legal authority to design or grant tax incentives, and only the Estonian Investment Agency and Innovation Norway have this authority for non-tax incentives.

Figure 2.5. OECD IPAs focus more on providing information, advocacy and advice than on designing and granting incentives

Role of OECD IPAs in incentives governance (as reported by IPAs)

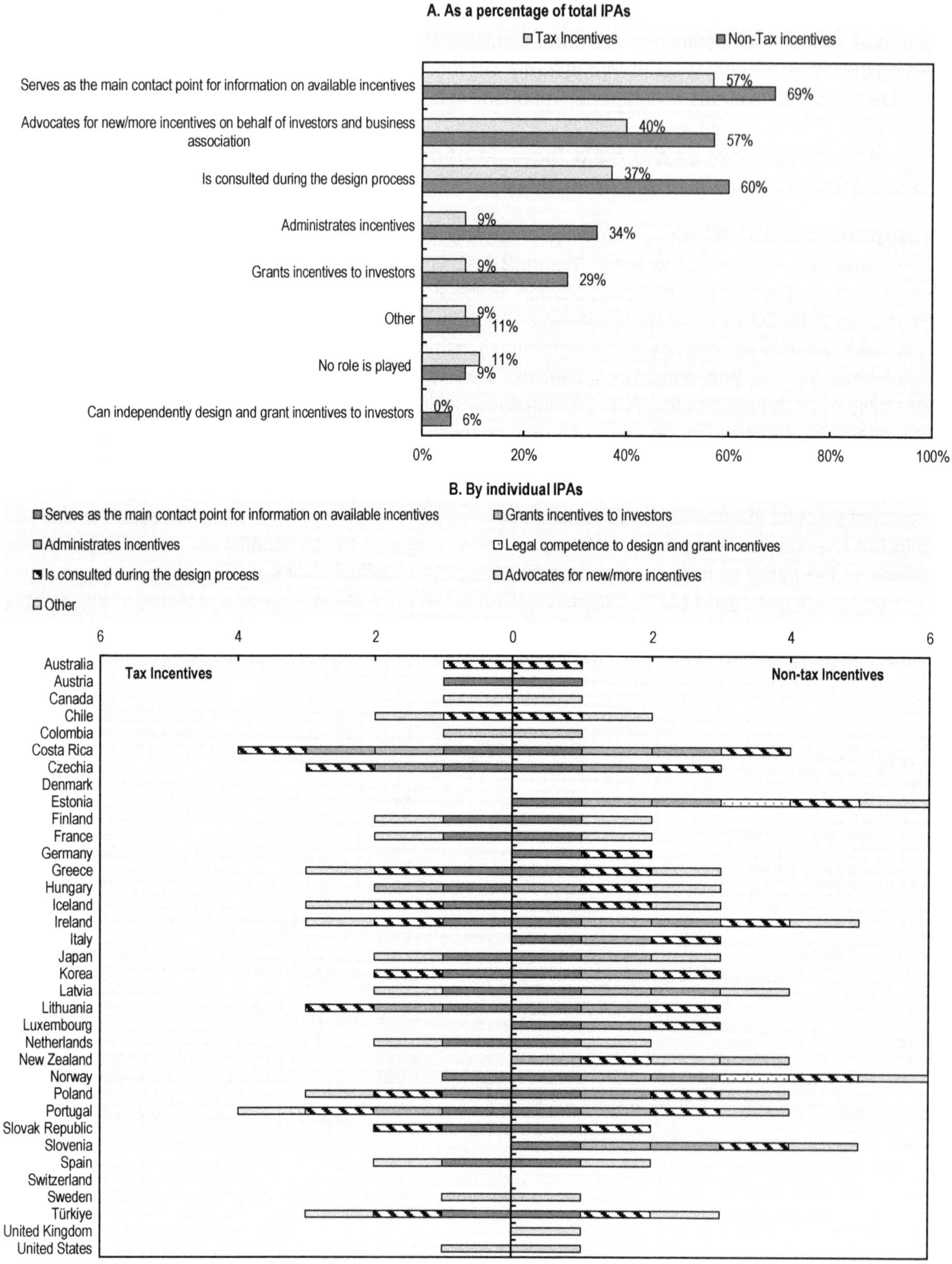

Source: OECD Survey on Investment Promotion and Investment Incentives, 2024.

The involvement of IPAs in the governance of investment incentives and the importance of these incentives in investment promotion influence each other. Survey evidence shows that IPAs that engage in a broader range of incentives-related activities – such as serving as the main contact point, advocating for additional incentives, participating in the design, administration and granting of incentives – are more likely to view investment incentives as essential tools for attracting FDI (Figure 2.6). Although the correlation coefficient is not particularly strong, the tendency is particularly noticeable for CIT incentives.

Figure 2.6. A higher number of incentives-related functions performed by IPAs is associated with a greater importance placed on incentives

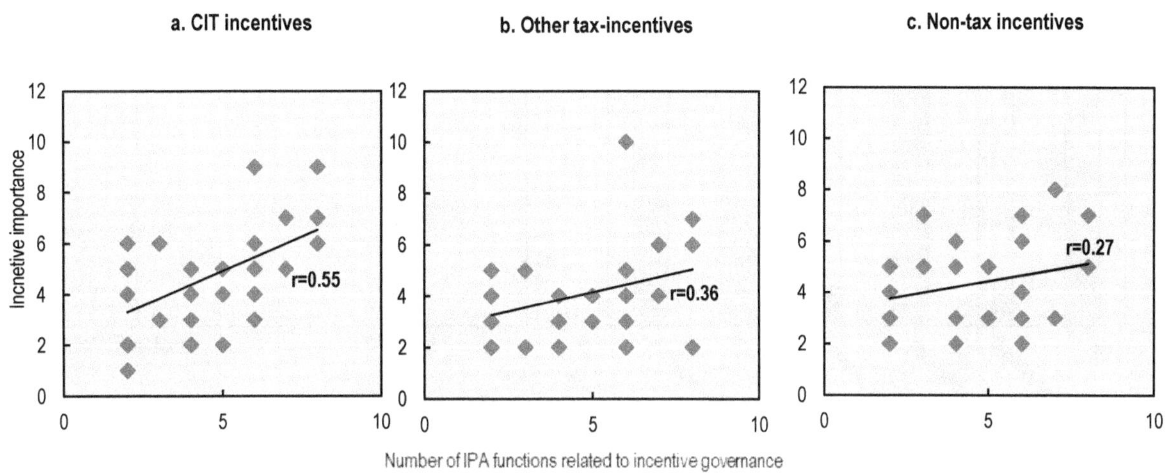

Source: OECD Survey on Investment Promotion and Investment Incentives, 2024.

Countries can adopt various institutional arrangements to manage the application processes for investment incentives, including reviewing applications, providing approvals and ensuring compliance with legal requirements. While IPAs primarily serve as promoters and information providers, they still play either a leading or a secondary role in the granting of incentives in 70% of cases (Figure 2.7.A). Additionally, while finance ministries are the lead entities only in less than 10% of cases, two-thirds of IPAs indicate that other ministries act as the main counterparts for investors applying for incentives, namely economic, industry, trade or sector-specific ministries. Subnational authorities are also important actors in the management of applications, as they are the lead authorities in 35% of OECD countries and involved in another 35%. This is the case, for example of Türkiye's regional development agencies or the local government agencies or major offices in Colombia. Finally, 34% of IPAs identified other entities as the main authorities, such as the tax administration agencies in Finland and Iceland or the Austrian federal development and financing bank in Austria.

When investors seek to apply for investment incentives, they must often engage with several actors throughout the process. All surveyed IPAs from OECD countries indicate that investors must interact with various entities to secure incentives, suggesting a lack of centralised application procedures. On average, each country has 1.85 lead entities and 1.5 additional entities involved (Figure 2.7.B). This fragmentation can make the application process more complex and time-consuming for investors compared to a centralised system with a single point of contact as can be found in some jurisdictions (Box 2.2).

Figure 2.7. Investors typically need to engage with multiple actors to apply for investment incentives, while IPA roles differ across jurisdictions

OECD government institutions' role in granting incentives (as reported by IPAs)

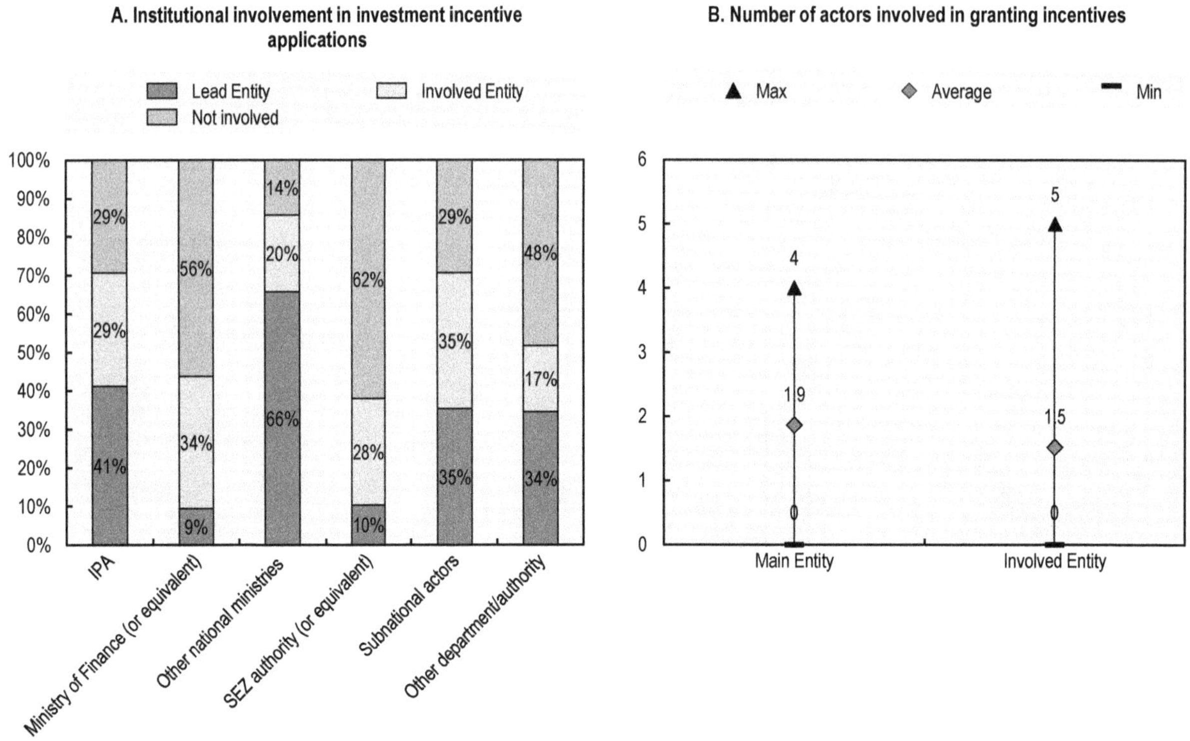

Source: OECD Survey on Investment Promotion and Investment Incentives, 2024.

Box 2.2. IPA centralised process for the granting of investment incentives: the example of Poland

In Poland, investors seeking incentives initially contact the Polish Investment and Trade Agency (PAIH), the national IPA, which conducts a preliminary screening to assess their eligibility for investment incentives. PAIH evaluates the firms' data and determines eligibility for specific incentives.

With regard to the governmental grant, PAIH based on the information obtained from investors, prepares a project description. This description includes an assessment of the investment and the proposed amount of support, along with a justification. The completed description, along with supporting documents, is then submitted by PAIH to the Ministry of Economy. An interministerial committee reviews the application and recommends a grant amount, after which the ministry makes the final decision. The investor has 30 days to accept the proposed support and, if accepted, an agreement is concluded.

Source: Polish Investment and Trade Agency (2024[57]), Investment incentives, https://www.paih.gov.pl/en/why_poland/investment_incentives/governmental_grants/

2.2.2. *The coexistence of subnational and national incentives and the degree of decentralisation can influence how subnational authorities govern them*

As mentioned previously, subnational authorities often play a significant role in the governance of incentives, particularly in countries with high levels of decentralised spending and taxation. These roles could involve evaluating applications and awarding incentives, overseeing compliance with incentive agreements, or developing policies for incentives. When OECD countries are grouped by decentralisation models and forms of state – whether unitary or federal – a distinct pattern emerges. In federal countries, there is a higher proportion of subnational IPAs with multiple roles related to incentives (Figure 2.8.A). In contrast, unitary countries have a higher proportion of subnational IPAs with little or no involvement in incentives. This trend also holds when considering the OECD's typology based on fiscal indicators (Figure 2.8.B). In highly decentralised countries, subnational IPAs are more active in the governance of incentives, with all such countries involving subnational entities in this process. This contrasts sharply with low-decentralisation countries, where subnational authorities are not involved in incentive governance in 56% of cases, highlighting a clear divide based on the level of decentralisation.

Figure 2.8. In decentralised countries, subnational authorities tend to have a greater degree of involvement in the governance of incentives

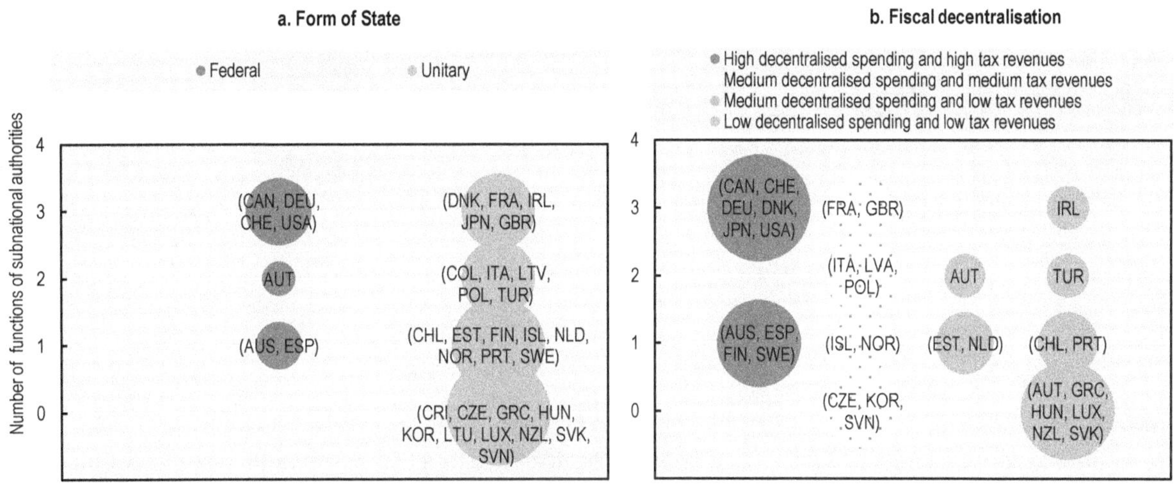

Note: In the case of fiscal decentralisation (Panel B), four categorised of countries are based on their levels of decentralised spending and tax revenues.
Source: OECD elaboration based on (OECD, 2019[58]) and OECD Survey on Investment Promotion and Investment Incentives, 2024.

This decentralised approach allows subnational authorities to play varying roles in the design, granting and administration of investment incentives, ranging from policy development to compliance oversight. The survey highlights that, in 60% of cases, IPAs identified the evaluation of applications and the awarding of incentives as the most prominent role of subnational authorities (Figure 2.9.A). Design and compliance oversight were also significant, with both mentioned in 40% of cases. Subnational authorities are not involved in the governance of incentives in all OECD countries, as they do not participate in this process in 9 out of 35 countries.

Subnational incentives can be offered either in co-ordination with, or independently of, national incentives. This local-level decision making ensures that incentives are effectively targeted and responds to regional needs. While 17% of OECD countries do not offer subnational incentives, the remaining 83% do (Figure 2.9.B). When subnational incentives are offered, they are done so in co-ordination with national incentives in most cases (28%) to avoid overlap. Conversely, in 20% of cases, subnational governments choose their incentives at their own discretion and, in another 20% of countries, incentives are designed or applied differently across various regions. In only 9% of countries, regions offer the same incentives than to those available at the national level.

Figure 2.9. While subnational incentives are rarely offered in co-ordination with national incentives, subnational authorities are often involved in the granting of incentives

As a percentage of respondents (as reported by IPAs)

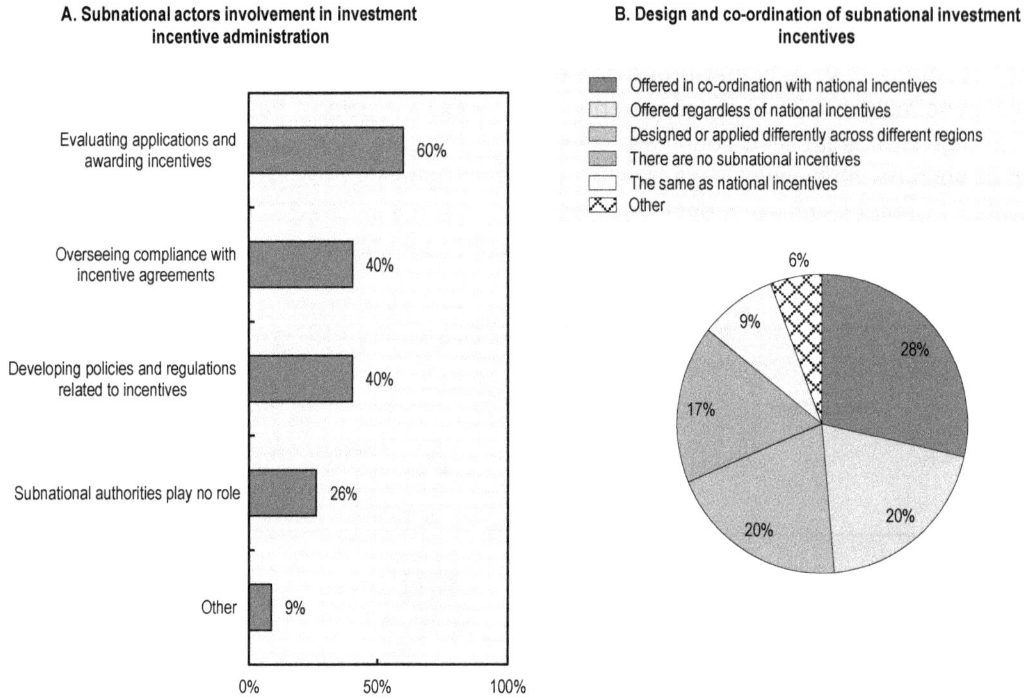

Source: OECD Survey on Investment Promotion and Investment Incentives, 2024.

Navigating this complex landscape of national and subnational investment incentives, governed by different laws, can be time-consuming and challenging for investors. To address this, some countries are introducing tools to streamline the process, helping investors navigate complex financial support options, minimise upfront costs, and accelerate the timeline to profitability (Box 2.3).

Box 2.3. US states business incentives database and target industries dashboard

In addition to federal incentives, US states also offer investment incentives. To help investors identify the most relevant incentives, SelectUSA has implemented the state business incentives database, a one-stop resource for information about incentive programmes in all 50 states. The database, which currently contains information on 2 438 programmes offered across states, provides information on programme description, objectives, and eligibility requirements.

SelectUSA has also developed the Target Industries Dashboard, a tool designed for international investors seeking to establish operations in the United States. The dashboard displays the US states and territories where different industries are prioritised and includes links to each state's fact sheet and state sectoral incentives database page.

Source: C2ER (2024[59]), State Business Incentives Database, https://www.stateincentives.org/; and SelectUSA (2024[60]), Target Industries Dashboard, https://www.trade.gov/selectusa-target-industries-dashboard.

2.2.3. Informal collaboration between IPAs and other agencies is a common practice to align incentives with policy goals and facilitate implementation

Despite the involvement of different entities in the governance of incentives, IPAs' interinstitutional co-ordination with national and subnational agencies tend to be informal. The institutional governance of investment incentives involves numerous ministries and agencies at the national and subnational levels, requiring effective co-ordination throughout the incentive ecosystem. As investment is a horizontal policy involving many institutions, collaboration is central to successful investment promotion efforts, with IPAs often playing a co-ordinating role between investors and various regional partners (Lewis and Whyte, 2022[51]). The survey reveals that most IPAs co-ordinate effectively to align incentive policy goals and ensure effective implementation, but informal mechanisms are prevalent (Figure 2.10). National IPAs have informal co-ordination mechanisms with national institutions in three-quarters of cases and with subnational institutions in half of cases. IPAs participate to a lesser extent in formal mechanisms, with 47% engaging formally with national actors and only 24% with subnational actors.

Figure 2.10. The co-ordination of IPAs with government entities is mostly informal, both at national and subnational levels

Percentage of OECD countries with IPAs participating in incentives co-ordination mechanisms (as reported by IPAs)

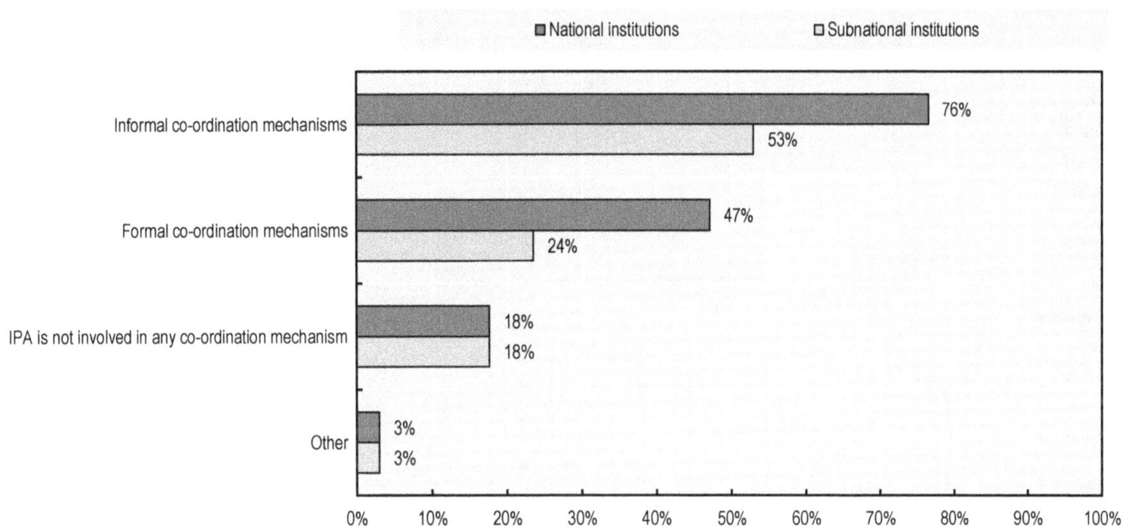

Source: OECD Survey on Investment Promotion and Investment Incentives, 2024.

Despite the engagement of many IPAs in incentive co-ordination mechanisms, 18% of them – namely ABA Invest in Austria, Business Finland, the Hungarian Investment Promotion Agency, the Netherlands Foreign Investment Agency, Business Sweden, and Switzerland Global Enterprise – do not participate in either formal or informal co-ordination with subnational or national institutions (Table 2.4). The risk of limited co-ordination is that incentives may overlap, be inconsistent or even work at cross-purposes (IMF, OECD, UN, World Bank, 2015[24]).

Table 2.4. Participation of IPAs in incentive co-ordination mechanisms with government entities

Country	Formal co-ordination		Informal co-ordination mechanisms		Not involved	
	National institutions	Subnational institutions	National institutions	Subnational institutions	National institutions	Subnational institutions
Australia						
Austria						
Chile						
Colombia						
Costa Rica						
Czechia						
Denmark						
Estonia						
Finland						
France						
Germany						
Greece						
Hungary						
Iceland						
Ireland						
Italy						
Japan						
Korea						
Latvia						
Lithuania						
Luxembourg						
Netherlands						
New Zealand						
Norway						
Poland						
Portugal						
Slovak Republic						
Slovenia						
Spain						
Sweden						
Switzerland						
Türkiye						
United Kingdom						
United States						

Note: Coloured cells indicate the presence of a co-ordination mechanism. The IPA of Spain has a different type of co-ordination mechanism, which consist of ex-post controls to avoid overlapping of incentives.
Source: OECD Survey on Investment Promotion and Investment Incentives, 2024.

2.2.4. Other government agencies often play a more prominent role in monitoring and evaluating incentives than IPAs

The participation of IPAs in the M&E of investment incentives is limited compared to other government entities. Monitoring tracks intervention progress over time, while evaluation examines incentives' implementation, effectiveness and outcome achievement. A better understanding of whether investment incentives contribute to policy goals, and at what costs, requires comprehensive M&E (OECD, 2024[34]). According to the survey results, government entities are involved in 89% of monitoring activities and 91% of evaluation activities, while IPAs are involved in only 54% and 40% of these activities, respectively (Figure 2.11.A).

Despite their limited role, IPAs' position as intermediaries between the government and investors allows them to participate moderately in some M&E activities. For example, 57% of IPAs request feedback from investors on incentives, which is the only activity where IPAs are not overshadowed by other parts of government given their direct interaction with investors (Figure 2.11.B and Figure 2.11.C). About a third of agencies also register the take-up of incentives, type and number of benefits granted per beneficiary, an activity which is nonetheless much more frequently conducted by policymakers (in 80% of countries). CzechInvest serves as a prime example of an agency conducting monitoring activities through its dedicated dashboard (Box 2.4). While IPAs are moderately involved in some monitoring activities – although to a much smaller extent than other parts of government – the difference is particularly striking for evaluation activities. For example, 71% of governments entities conduct cost-benefit analysis of incentives while only 17% of IPAs do so. The same proportions apply when it comes to assessing whether the policy objectives of incentives are met. Two-thirds of OECD governments assess the impact of incentives in specific regions, an activity consistent with the policy goals of many governments to support regional development (see first part of the paper).

Box 2.4. CzechInvest Dashboard on Investment incentives Statistics

CzechInvest has recently launched a dashboard that consolidates statistics on investment incentives. This dashboard provides up-to-date information on the incentives granted, categorised by sectors, type of investment projects, and country of applicant, as well as by region. It includes data on supported projects, total investment, and jobs created. Additionally, the dashboard offers granular information about the supported companies, detailing their investments, the jobs created, and the type of incentives granted, such as tax incentives, in-kind support like land, or financial incentives such as capital cash grants, grants for retraining among others.

Source: Czechinvest (2024[61]), Investment Incentives Statistics, https://www.czechinvest.org/en/For-Investors/Investment-Incentives.

Figure 2.11. IPAs tend to participate less in M&E activities compared to other government agencies and ministries

Role of OECD IPAs in M&E of investment incentives (as reported by IPAs)

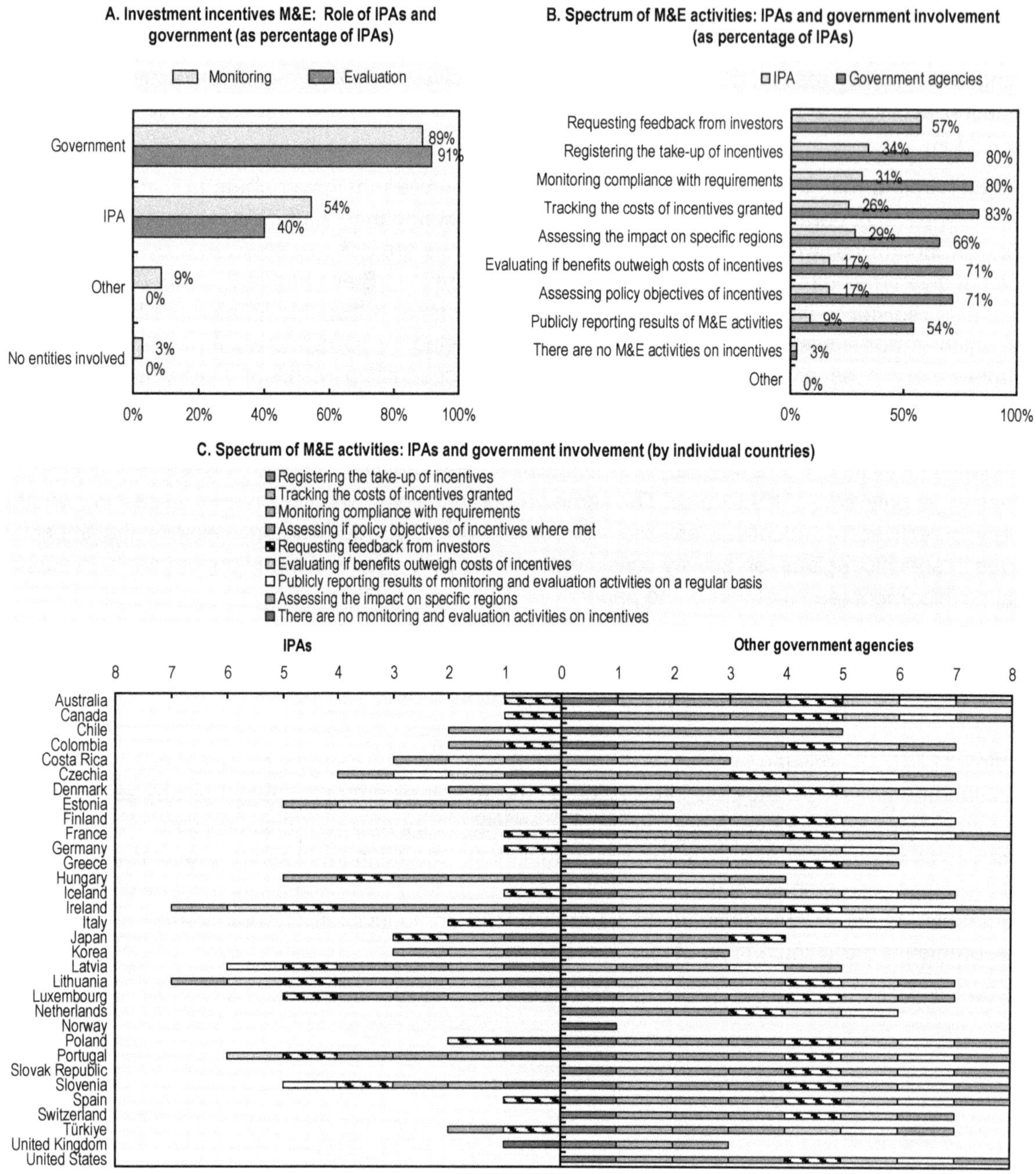

Source: OECD Survey on Investment Promotion and Investment Incentives, 2024.

Note

[1] The GMT aims to establish a 15% effective corporate tax rate for MNEs groups with annual revenues exceeding EUR 750 million. This measure addresses ongoing concerns about profit shifting, harmful tax competition, and a downward race in corporate tax rates. If an MNE's ETR in a jurisdiction falls below 15%, and it does not have strong substance in the jurisdiction (employment and tangible assets), it may be subject to top-up taxes under the Global Anti-Base Erosion (GloBE) Rules, a key component of Pillar Two of the OECD/G20 Inclusive Framework on Base Erosion and Profit Shifting (BEPS). Pillar Two will discourage MNEs from engaging in profit shifting and help countries achieve a better balance between attracting investment through tax policies and mobilising domestic revenues. Adopted by over 135 countries in 2021, the two-pillar solution addresses the tax challenges posed by the globalised and digitalised economy. As of 2024, around 60 jurisdictions are actively implementing the GMT.

References

Andersen, M., B. Kett and E. von Uexkull (2018), *Corporate tax incentives and FDI in developing* [8]
countries., 2017/2018 Global Investment Competitiveness Report: Foreign Investor Perspectives and Policy Implications,Global Investment Competitiveness Report: Foreign Investor Perspectives and Policy Implications 1, https://hdl.handle.net/10986/28493.

Aust, V., A. Morais and I. Pinto (2020), “How does foreign direct investment contribute to [21]
Sustainable Development Goals? Evidence from African countries”, *Journal of Cleaner Production*, Vol. 245, p. 118823, https://doi.org/10.1016/j.jclepro.2019.118823.

Bobenič Hintošová, A., F. Sudzina and T. Barlašová (2021), “Direct and Indirect Effects of [17]
Investment Incentives in Slovakia”, *Journal of Risk and Financial Management*, Vol. 14/2, p. 56, https://doi.org/10.3390/jrfm14020056.

C2ER (2024), “State Business Incentives Database”, https://www.stateincentives.org/. [59]

Celani, A., L. Dressler and T. Hanappi (2022), “Assessing tax relief from targeted investment tax [18]
incentives through corporate effective tax rates: Methodology and initial findings for seven Sub-Saharan African countries”, *OECD Taxation Working Papers*, No. 58, OECD Publishing, Paris, https://doi.org/10.1787/3eaddf88-en.

Celani, A., L. Dressler and M. Wermelinger (2022), “Building an Investment Tax Incentives [2]
database: Methodology and initial findings for 36 developing countries”, *OECD Working Papers on International Investment*, No. 2022/01, OECD Publishing, Paris, https://doi.org/10.1787/62e075a9-en.

Charlton, A. and N. Davis (2007), “Does Investment Promotion Work?”, *The B.E. Journal of* [47]
Economic Analysis & Policy, Vol. 7/1, https://doi.org/10.2202/1935-1682.1743.

Christiansen, H., C. Oman and A. Charlton (2003), “Incentives-based Competition for Foreign [39]
Direct Investment: The Case of Brazil”, *OECD Working Papers on International Investment*, No. 2003/1, OECD Publishing, Paris, https://doi.org/10.1787/631632456403.

Cuervo-Cazurra, A., B. Silva-Rêgo and A. Figueira (2022), “Financial and fiscal incentives and [28]
inward foreign direct investment: When quality institutions substitute incentives”, *Journal of International Business Policy*, Vol. 5/4, pp. 417-443, https://doi.org/10.1057/s42214-021-00130-9.

Czechinvest (2024), “Investment Incentives Statistics”, https://www.czechinvest.org/en/For- [61]
Investors/Investment-Incentives.

Dama, A., G. Rota-Graziosi and F. Sawadogo (2024), "The regressivity of CIT exemptions in Africa", *International Tax and Public Finance*, Vol. 31/3, pp. 909-934, https://doi.org/10.1007/s10797-023-09825-6. [23]

Danzman, S. and A. Slaski (2021), "Explaining deference: why and when do policymakers think FDI needs tax incentives?", *Review of International Political Economy*, Vol. 29/4, pp. 1085-1111, https://doi.org/10.1080/09692290.2021.1885475. [5]

Echandi, R., J. Krajcovicova and C. Qiang (2015), *The Impact of Investment Policy in a Changing Global Economy: a Review of the Literature*, World Bank Policy Research Working Paper No. 7437, https://papers.ssrn.com/sol3/papers.cfm?abstract_id=2673878. [22]

Elysée (2024), "Choose France", https://www.elysee.fr/emmanuel-macron/choose-france. [53]

fDi intelligence (2023), *Global competition for climate investment heats up*, https://www.fdiintelligence.com/content/data-trends/global-competition-for-climate-investment-heats-up-82517. [46]

FitzGerald, V. (2002), *Regulatory investment incentives*, http://workingpapers.qeh.ox.ac.uk/RePEc/qeh/qehwps/qehwps80.pdf. [32]

Guceri, I. and M. Albinowski (2021), "Investment responses to tax policy under uncertainty", *Journal of Financial Economics*, Vol. 141/3, pp. 1147-1170, https://doi.org/10.1016/j.jfineco.2021.04.032. [16]

Guceri, I. and L. Liu (2019), "Effectiveness of Fiscal Incentives for R&D: Quasi-experimental Evidence", *American Economic Journal: Economic Policy*, Vol. 11/1, pp. 266-291, https://doi.org/10.1257/pol.20170403. [14]

Harding, T. and B. Javorcik (2012), "Investment Promotion and FDI Inflows: Quality Matters", *CESifo Economic Studies*, Vol. 59/2, pp. 337-359, https://doi.org/10.1093/cesifo/ifs029. [9]

Havránek, T. and Z. Iršová (2010), *On the intensity of international subsidy competition for FDI.*, Theoretical and Applied Economics 17: 25–54., https://www.researchgate.net/publication/41890710_On_the_Intensity_of_International_Subsidy_Competition_for_FDI. [10]

Hintošová, A. and &. Barlašová (2021), *The Role Of Investment Promotion Policy In Attracting Foreign Direct Investment: The Case Of Slovakia,*, Public administration issues, Higher School of Economics,, pp. 27-40., https://ideas.repec.org/a/nos/vgmu00/2021i5p27-40.html. [30]

Huq, T. et al. (2024), "The takeover Tango: Unraveling the impact of state-owned enterprise acquisitions on American competitors", *Research in International Business and Finance*, Vol. 68, p. 102167, https://doi.org/10.1016/j.ribaf.2023.102167. [43]

IMF, OECD, UN, World Bank (2015), *Options for Low Income Countries' Effective and Efficient Use of Tax Incentives for Investment*, https://www.tax-platform.org/sites/pct/files/publications/100756-Tax-incentives-Main-report-options-PUBLIC_0.pdf. [24]

James, S. (2013), "Effectiveness of Tax and Non-Tax Incentives and Investments: Evidence and Policy Implications", *SSRN Electronic Journal*, https://doi.org/10.2139/ssrn.2401905. [4]

JETRO (2024), "Invest Japan Hotline", https://www.jetro.go.jp/en/invest/jetros_support/hotline/. [54]

Johnson, L. and P. Toledano (2022), *Investment Incentives: A Survey of Policies and Approaches for Sustainable Investment*, https://scholarship.law.columbia.edu/sustainable_investment/2/. [27]

Katitas, A. and S. Pandya (2024), "Investment incentives attract foreign direct investment: evidence from the great recession", *Public Choice*, https://doi.org/10.1007/s11127-024-01158-0. [49]

Kobayashi, Y. and N. Daigo (2016), , https://ideas.repec.org/p/eti/rdpsjp/16007.html. [26]

Lewis, P. and R. Whyte (2022), *The Role of Subnational Investment Promotion Agencies*, http://documents.worldbank.org/curated/en/099245210012218194/P17553808bd2a306a090420a272cf45ddc6. [51]

Maffini, G., J. Xing and M. Devereux (2019), "The Impact of Investment Incentives: Evidence from UK Corporation Tax Returns", *American Economic Journal: Economic Policy*, Vol. 11/3, pp. 361-389, https://doi.org/10.1257/pol.20170254. [12]

OECD (2024), *Key takeaways from the 2023-2024 PMR indicators*, https://issuu.com/oecd.publishing/docs/key_takeaways_from_the_2023-2024_update_of_the_oec. [31]

OECD (2024), *Summary: Economic Impact Assessment of the Global Minimum Tax (January 2024)*, https://www.oecd.org/content/dam/oecd/en/topics/policy-issues/cross-border-and-international-tax/summary-economic-impact-assessment-global-minimum-tax-january-2024.pdf. [56]

OECD (2024), *Sustainable Investment Policy Perspectives in the Economic Community of West African States (ECOWAS)*, OECD Publishing, Paris, https://doi.org/10.1787/654e2de5-en. [34]

OECD (2023), "Improving transparency of incentives for investment facilitation", *OECD Business and Finance Policy Papers*, No. 35, OECD Publishing, Paris, https://doi.org/10.1787/ab40a2f1-en. [3]

OECD (2023), *Investment tax incentives in mena: design and policy goals*, https://www.oecd.org/mena/eu-oecd-mediterranean-investment/Investment%20tax%20incentives%20in%20MENA_insights%20from%20OECD%20ITID.pdf. [38]

OECD (2023), *Policy Toolkit for Strengthening FDI and SME Linkages*, OECD Publishing, Paris, https://doi.org/10.1787/688bde9a-en. [42]

OECD (2023), *Rethinking Regional Attractiveness in the New Global Environment*, OECD Regional Development Studies, OECD Publishing, Paris, https://doi.org/10.1787/a9448db4-en. [48]

OECD (2022), *FDI Qualities Policy Toolkit*, OECD Publishing, Paris, https://doi.org/10.1787/7ba74100-en. [20]

OECD (2022), *Financing Growth and Turning Data into Business: Helping SMEs Scale Up*, OECD Studies on SMEs and Entrepreneurship, OECD Publishing, Paris, https://doi.org/10.1787/81c738f0-en. [40]

OECD (2022), *OECD Investment Tax Incentives Database – 2022 Update: Tax incentives for sustainable development*, https://www.oecd.org/investment/investment-policy/oecd-investment-tax-incentives-database-2022-update-brochure.pdf. [1]

OECD (2022), "Recommendation of the Council on Foreign Direct Investment Qualities for Sustainable Development", *OECD Legal Instruments*, OECD/LEGAL/0476, OECD, Paris, https://legalinstruments.oecd.org/en/instruments/OECD-LEGAL-0476. [19]

OECD (2022), *Recommendation of the Council on Foreign Direct Investment Qualities for Sustainable Development*, https://legalinstruments.oecd.org/en/instruments/OECD-LEGAL-0476. [36]

OECD (2022), *Tax Incentives and the Global Minimum Corporate Tax: Reconsidering Tax Incentives after the GloBE Rules*, OECD Publishing, Paris, https://doi.org/10.1787/25d30b96-en. [55]

OECD (2022), "The geography of foreign investment in OECD member countries: How investment promotion agencies support regional development", *OECD Business and Finance Policy Papers*, No. 20, OECD Publishing, Paris, https://doi.org/10.1787/1f293a25-en. [45]

OECD (2021), "Towards smarter use of investment incentives", in *Middle East and North Africa Investment Policy Perspectives*, OECD Publishing, Paris, https://doi.org/10.1787/813bef22-en. [11]

OECD (2020), *Regulatory Impact Assessment*, OECD Best Practice Principles for Regulatory Policy, OECD Publishing, Paris, https://doi.org/10.1787/7a9638cb-en. [37]

OECD (2020), "The effects of R&D tax incentives and their role in the innovation policy mix: Findings from the OECD microBeRD project, 2016-19", *OECD Science, Technology and Industry Policy Papers*, No. 92, OECD Publishing, Paris, https://doi.org/10.1787/65234003-en. [29]

OECD (2019), *Making Decentralisation Work: A Handbook for Policy-Makers*, OECD Multi-level Governance Studies, OECD Publishing, Paris, https://doi.org/10.1787/g2g9faa7-en. [58]

OECD (2018), "Towards an international framework for investment facilitation", *OECD Business and Finance Policy Papers*, No. 47, OECD Publishing, Paris, https://doi.org/10.1787/b82771dc-en. [52]

OECD (2015), *Policy Framework for Investment, 2015 Edition*, OECD Publishing, Paris, https://doi.org/10.1787/9789264208667-en. [50]

OECD (2012), *Competitive Neutrality: Maintaining a Level Playing Field between Public and Private Business*, OECD Publishing, Paris, https://doi.org/10.1787/9789264178953-en. [44]

OECD (Forthcoming), *Tax incentive policymaking: a practical guide.* [35]

Polish Investment and Trade Agency (2024), *Investment incentives*, https://www.paih.gov.pl/en/why_poland/investment_incentives/governmental_grants/. [57]

SelectUSA (2024), "Target Industries Dashboard", https://www.trade.gov/selectusa-target-industries-dashboard. [60]

Sungur, O. (2019), "Spatial Distribution of Investment Incentives and the Impact of New Incentive System for Less Developed Regions in Turkey", *Review of Economic Perspectives*, Vol. 19/1, pp. 25-48, https://doi.org/10.2478/revecp-2019-0002. [15]

Tuomi, K. (2012), *Review of investment incentives. Best Practice and Attracting Investments*, IGC International Growth Centre, https://www.theigc.org/sites/default/files/2012/06/Tuomi-2012-Working-Paper.pdf. [6]

UNCTAD (2024), *Promoting International Investment by Small and Medium-sized Enterprises*, https://unctad.org/system/files/official-document/diae2023d7_en.pdf. [41]

World Bank Group (2018), *Global Investment Competitiveness Report 2017/2018: Foreign Investor Perspectives and Policy Implications*, http://hdl.handle.net/10986/28493. [7]

WTO (2023), *Trade Policy Review: Türkiye*, https://www.wto.org/english/tratop_e/tpr_e/tp539_e.htm. [33]

Zhang, C., L. Chen and H. Song (2022), "The impact of social security contributions on corporate innovation: evidence from the contribution collection reform in China", *Applied Economics*, Vol. 54/46, pp. 5320-5334, https://doi.org/10.1080/00036846.2022.2042480. [25]

Zwick, E. and J. Mahon (2017), "Tax Policy and Heterogeneous Investment Behavior", *American Economic Review*, Vol. 107/1, pp. 217-248, https://doi.org/10.1257/aer.20140855. [13]

www.ingramcontent.com/pod-product-compliance
Lightning Source LLC
Chambersburg PA
CBHW061225240926
51846CB00006B/1360
* 9 7 8 9 2 6 4 3 8 8 5 9 8 *